SAILING
ON THE EDGE

AMERICA'S CUP®

WRITTEN BY

Bob Fisher, Kimball Livingston, Ivor Wilkins,
Mark Chisnell, & James Boyd

INTRODUCTION BY

Roger Vaughan

PHOTOGRAPHS BY

Carlo Borlenghi, Chris Cameron, Daniel Forster,
Sharon Green, Guilain Grenier, Bob Grieser,
Gilles Martin-Raget, Dan Nerney, & Sander van der Borch

INSIGHT EDITIONS

San Rafael, California

• CONTENTS •

THE CREW HAD FELT THE BOWS DIG IN BEFORE . . .

THEY WERE FAMILIAR WITH THE SENSATION of the sterns rising out of the water as the bows buried under tons of water rushing past at up to 40 knots.

Turning downwind in the new America's Cup catamaran class requires nerves of steel. It's when the towering, powerful wing sail is broadest to the wind. Every piece of equipment on the yacht strains under the added pressure of the wind against the broad surface area. It's a moment that puts an empty feeling in the pit of the stomach of the sailors—a weird sensation that catches one's attention.

The ORACLE TEAM USA crew became acutely aware that this turn downwind had strayed from the norm when skipper Jimmy Spithil yelled, "Keep an eye on your mates!" Moments later, many of the sailors aboard were quite literally swimming for their lives. Hours later, as the overturned platform was being swept westward into a setting sun by an ebb tide, the team could still be seen struggling to recoup all that they could from the once sleek, 72-foot "cat."

The 2013 America's Cup represents an ambitious rethinking of every facet of the centuries old event. A new design rule that features, for the first time, wing sail catamarans was introduced. The powerful, light boats demand a new breed of sailor; physical prowess and vast reserves of courage are the new currency. The use of a catamaran and its shallow draft allows the racecourse to be placed close to shore, in plain view of spectators sitting in shoreside bleachers or on rocky outcrops. The racing has even been made more appealing to the television viewer, with graphics indicating positioning overlaid in real time on the broadcast picture. The changes were met with great fanfare at America's Cup World Series regattas, turning skeptics into supports around the world.

But the ORACLE TEAM USA capsize punctuated these incredible changes with the very real possibility of disaster. Would the new-look America's Cup, with its high-speed, high-risk, high-tech, high-visibility ethos work? For the challengers, the answer lay in rising to unprecedented demands. For the authors of the revolution, at stake in the answer was nothing less than everything.

THE AMERICA'S CUP AS EXTREME SPORT

ROGER VAUGHAN

N 1820, A STRANGE THING HAPPENED. A MAN NAMED JOHN Cox Stevens took delivery of a catamaran he had commissioned as his private yacht. He named it *Double Trouble*. This was noteworthy because private yachts were a rarity in 1820. Catamarans in those days were even rarer. It turned out to be a significant event, because in 1844, Stevens would found the New York Yacht Club and become its first commodore. In 1850, he would become the driving force behind the syndicate that caused the schooner *America* to be designed, built, and sailed across the Atlantic to challenge the British to a boat race. After *America* won that race, he would rename the large silver ewer he won "The America's Cup" and take the lead in writing a deed of gift for a yacht race inviting "friendly competition between foreign countries."

In several ways, John Cox Stevens solidly set the stage for the past 162 years of America's Cup competition that would culminate in 2013 with a match between 72-foot catamarans. First of all, the whole concept of *America* was outrageous. In 1851, not only were the British perceived to rule the waves militarily and in yachting, but a scant thirty-seven years had passed since they burned Washington, D.C., during the War of 1812. Stevens was a successful businessman from a prominent family. A known gambler, he was by all accounts a smart, aggressive, confident man. And he had an agenda: to promote the design and ship-building prowess of the United States. Stevens cut the path for men of his ilk to follow, and follow they did through thirty-three challenges. Without exception, those who have sought to fund competitions for the America's Cup have been among the wealthiest and most powerful individuals in the world, from England's iron and steel baron James Ashbury, Earl of Dunraven, and aviation pioneer T.O.M. Sopwith to Ireland's tea magnate Sir Thomas Lipton, Italy's fashion maestro Patrizio Bertelli, and Australia's real estate tycoon Alan Bond. American defenders have included familiar names like Vanderbilt, Cunningham, Turner, Koch, and Ellison.

Embracing tippy racing multihulls that skim the surface and are more at home on a beach than at a dock was a tough order for traditionalists. For 152 years, the America's Cup was contested in monohulls that rarely pushed the speed dial over 14 knots. Although there have been gear failures (spars breaking, sails tearing—even a sinking), no boat in the Cup's history has ever capsized. With two notable exceptions aside, for more than 160 years, the Cup has been the epitome of traditional yachting. For many of those years, it was complete with white flannels, navy yachting jackets, gold braid on the caps, and the observation of flag etiquette.

ABOVE: *Young America* buckled amidships and nearly sank to the bottom of the Hauraki Gulf in November 1999, during the Louis Vuitton Cup in New Zealand. • OPPOSITE: ORACLE TEAM USA Spithill pitchpoled after rouding a reach mark during an AC World Series fleet race, October 2012. Miraculously, there were no serious injuries.

FROM THE OUTSET, the 2013 America's Cup had an entirely new look. For all their speed and flash, large racing multihulls simply do not have the elegant, often majestic presence of monohulls. With hard wing sails emblazoned with eye-catching logos, with the wide stance of twin hulls that seem too frail, the boats have an experimental look. Wearing heavy-weave, flexible body suits, crash helmets, and life vests that look like pads under form-fitting tops, the crews resemble a cross between mountain climbers and bicycle racers. To those who had followed the event even in a casual way, the new America's Cup was as unrecognizable (unthinkable!) as the advent of blue courts, yellow balls, and colorful outfits were to those used to the green grass, red clay, and white balls and outfits of tennis.

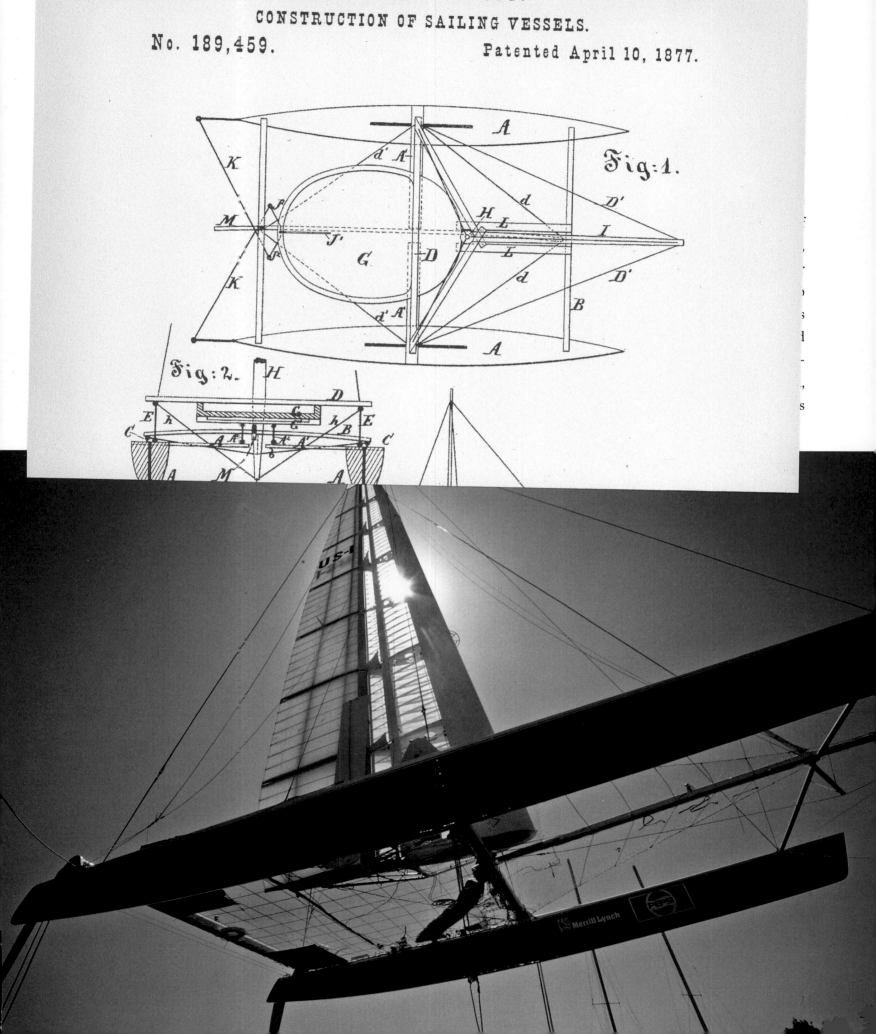

next defense that went several steps over the line. The Challenger of Record, BMW ORACLE Racing run by Larry Ellison, CEO of ORACLE, had no choice but to file legal objections. Two long years of legal wrangling went on between two of the world's wealthiest men. The most proficient attorneys available pitted their skills against one another. Ellison ultimately won 14 out of 15 judgments from the New York Supreme Court, though the match was settled on the water, not in the courtroom.

Ellison and Bertarelli still could not agree on the terms for the match. The parties had not settled on a boat, or even a formula for a boat to be used in the competition. When that impasse occurs, the Deed of Gift dictates the particulars. The resulting event is called a DOG (Deed of Gift) match. The boats must conform to a clause in the deed: Competing vessels "if of one mast shall not be less than 44-feet, nor more than 90-feet on the load waterline." The deed specifies the exact nature of courses for a three-race series.

Ellison and his troops at BMW ORACLE Racing were well into preparing a 90-foot waterline monohull for the match initially set for 2009 when they read a headline in the December 11, 2007, *Tribune de Genève*: "ALINGHI WILL DEFEND IN A MULTIHULL." That's when it all changed. The lesson learned in 1988 was plain: One simply doesn't elect to sail a monohull against a multihull.

The story, still untold at this point, of how BMW ORACLE scrapped its monohull project, refocused a bunch of monohull sailors on the theory and practice of racing multihulls, and recruited help from the best multihull sailors in the world, and how designers and builders took on a mission impossible to conceive and construct a large multihull in a fraction of the time that would be normally allotted for a project of that size—a 113-foot length overall multihull that would be competitive and also manageable for a crew of eight mere mortals—is almost beyond belief.

As if that weren't enough, a wing sail was added to the picture only six months before the match was to take place. Not only a wing sail, but at 223 feet, the tallest one ever built.

ABOVE: Luna Rossa's one-boat program left little room for error, but also allowed them to focus all their energy on the build of a single AC72.

he can go 16-plus knots upwind in a multihull? How can that sailor be happy going a maximum of 15 knots downwind in an America's Cup monohull when he can be scorching along at 40 downwind in a multihull? He can't. It was a no-brainer when it came to deciding whether to go back to racing monohulls in the 2013 Cup. When BMW ORACLE Racing's CEO, four-time America's Cup winner Russell Coutts, announced that the boat of choice would be a 72-foot catamaran, it was no surprise.

Given that only two teams had gone through a very expensive crash course that had advanced multihull/wing technology to a whole new level, defender BMW ORACLE Racing found itself in the unusual position of having to bring potential challengers up to speed. To do so, the AC45 catamaran was quickly conceived, designed, built, and sold to teams contemplating a challenge. There were nine takers (Alinghi was not among them). A schedule of AC45 racing was announced that saw teams racing for two years at locations beyond the 2013 host venue. Called the America's Cup World Series (ACWS), events took place in Portugal, England, Italy, and the United States. The events included fleet racing, the most popular format of racing in the sport, as well as match racing. For those not convinced that good match racing would be possible in multihulls known for their lack of mobility (slow to tack), and for their instant acceleration in puffs that tends to separate the boats on the racecourse, the ACWS was revealing.

What made the ACWS successful was creative thinking backed by leading-edge technological innovation. America's Cup Race Management, in particular Regatta Director Iain Murray, with John Craig and Mike Martin, conceived the reaching start, novel course formats, vastly simplified racing rules, umpiring by race officials ashore, and delineated course boundaries. All other sports have boundaries of some sort, but boundaries other than shallow water are a first in the history of yacht racing.

Stan Honey, director of technology for the America's Cup Event Authority, and his team were able to build AC LiveLine, the electronic system that gave life to the concepts. Honey, who brought us the yellow first-down line seen on televised NFL games, is a widely acclaimed racing sailor as well as an electrical engineering genius. The boundaries he and his team created are electronic. Television viewers see them as a superimposed graphic on their screens. Crews are alerted to their boat's proximity to a boundary by a flashing yellow light. If they "hit" a boundary, they are penalized (electronically) by judges sitting at consoles ashore, watching televised feeds from helicopters, chase boats, and race boats.

Boundaries not only keep the fleet centered on the course, which facilitates close-quarter racing for television coverage, but add a key tactical element to the racing. Boats with right-of-way must allow boats coming off the boundary room to maneuver, a condition burdened boats can use to their advantage.

The boundaries, along with the rest of the stunning graphic ensemble Honey's team produced—colored wakes to identify boats; lay lines (which show the optimum course to a mark); start and finish lines; grids showing distances between boats; three boat-length circles around marks indicating penalty areas—constitute a package that has made sailing as television and viewer friendly as it has ever been.

At a stroke, a sport in which boats are powered by invisible forces, in which competitors make decisions based on what the layman can't see—a sport governed by a complex and arcane set of rules—became understandable to the viewer. Better still, the multihulls' significantly increased speeds across the entire wind range meant that races were not only shorter but could be started reliably on time.

THE AC45S HAVE PROVED to be excellent trainers. Sailors love them. They are extremely fast and maneuverable, both tricky and rewarding to sail. Unlike the big multihulls of 2010 and the AC72s that followed, the AC45s have little instrumentation. Other than the AC LiveLine race management system they require seat-of-the-pants sailing. Crews had to learn how to set up controls on the wing by feel and experience. And the boats proved surprisingly robust. Several of the AC45s capsized as sailors tested the edges of performance, and they were repaired and back on the water the following day.

The AC45s also opened the America's Cup to a new breed of sailor. For years, heavy monohull classes and the match racing circuit have been predominant in funneling skippers into the America Cup ranks. Now skippers are coming from high-speed, athletic dinghies like the 49er and a variety of multihulls, from A- and C-Class to ORMA 60s. Another big difference: These sailors are younger. They had better be. The AC45s and AC72s are not your father's America's Cup yachts. What bronco busting is to rodeo, racing AC45s is to sailing. The crews are built like NFL linebackers and just as fit. Until 2010, the average age of a Cup skipper was thirty-eight. A quick poll of the America's Cup World Series skippers reduced that average by several years. The youngest among them was twenty-one.

Moving from the AC45s to the 72s was a significant leap for all the teams. One of the most impressive first looks at the AC72 was a video released by Emirates Team New Zealand that showed its boat hitting 35 knots. A chase boat, with four 300 hp outboards lashed to the transom at full crank, was struggling to keep up. At that speed, for a long, impossible moment, the 72's dagger foils lifted both hulls out of the water. The 72-foot, 13,000-pound catamaran under wing power was foiling. Seeing was believing.

Like the multihull behemoths from 2010 that helped orchestrate this sea change in the America's Cup, the 72s are technological marvels. Hundreds of

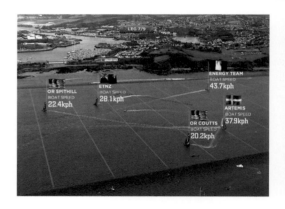

ALL ABOVE: AC LiveLine allowed television viewers to see course boundaries, boat speed, and penalties. • BELOW: Stan Honey displaying the Emmy Award won for his AC LiveLine technology package. • OPPOSITE: ORACLE TEAM USA during an AC72 training session in San Francisco Bay.

electronic strain gauges have been molded into the hulls and wings. All have readouts to help crews avoid what is called in auto racing "hitting the wall." Just as a driver's race is over after his car goes into the wall, if a crew capsizes an AC72 during a Cup race, there will be no tomorrow. Witness the extensive wing damage done when ORACLE TEAM USA's AC72 capsized while practicing in 25 knots of wind in October 2012. In a multihull, the maximum performance is outside the limit of what the boat can withstand. Therefore, crews in the 34th America's Cup finals must constantly recalibrate where they feel the edge is and how far they are prepared to go beyond it in order to win.

Reducing sail, throttling back, has always been a part of sailing in the interest of obtaining maximum boatspeed and control in strong winds. In offshore races, prudent skippers throttle back to avoid losing a mast. But the advent of 72-foot multihulls with fixed wings has made a crew's need to reduce power before crossing the line a do or crash-and-burn proposition. As we have seen, make a mistake, and it's over in the blink of an eye. ◄

TOP: ORACLE TEAM USA's Simeon Tienpont clinging onto the capsized 72 as the recovery team attempts to right the boat. • ABOVE: Luna Rossa Swordfish pushing its AC45 through heavy waters during the ACWS in Naples, Italy. • OPPOSITE: Emirates Team New Zealand flying on the foils of its first AC72.

A HISTORY OF CONTROVERSY & CONTENTION

BOB FISHER

The 1851 World's Fair in London was intended to establish Great Britain as the industrial leader of the world. The breakthrough event provided an opportunity for British manufacturers and inventors to display their superior products to other nations. It also set the stage for a group of upstart American yachtsmen to showcase their advancements in marine design and engineering. For the New York Yacht Club (NYYC), formed just seven years earlier, this international gathering presented the ideal moment to challenge the assumed authority of Great Britain's nautical power.

As fortune would have it, the Earl of Wilton, commodore of the Royal Yacht Squadron (RYS), had extended an invitation to the Americans to visit the Clubhouse at Cowes. There was no intimation of a challenge, but John Cox Stevens, a known gambler and the commodore of the NYYC, accepted in a competitive spirit. In his reply, he said that he and four or five friends had a yacht on the stocks that they hoped to launch in mid-April and "take with good grace the sound thrashing we are likely to get by venturing our longshore craft on your rough waters." Perhaps he was bluffing.

The previous November, Stevens and his associates—his brother Edwin, James Hamilton, George Schuyler, Hamilton Wilkes, and John Beekman Finlay—had received an offer from William Brown to build a yacht rigged for ocean sailing for $30,000 ($8 million today). The proposal came with a promise that he would take back the vessel without payment if it was not faster than any boat in the United States brought to compete with it. The gambling members of the NYYC could not refuse. Nor could the invitation from the British commodore have come at a better time—the NYYC syndicate wanted to win large wagers in England and wanted to do so before an international crowd.

Named *America,* the yacht was launched on May 3, 1851. To test Brown's promise, it was raced against the big sloop *Maria*—a flat-bottomed, scow-shaped centerboarder. The *Maria* easily outsailed *America,* which in turn outsailed all the other craft in the contest just as easily. The tests were held in smooth waters, and Brown believed they were inconclusive. Schuyler, too, admitted that the two boats were nearly matched, and the builders of *America* felt confident that new spars of proper dimensions and some alteration of sails would bring a different result.

Schuyler wrote to Brown: "I will give you $20,000 in cash for the yacht, finished as per contract, equipped and ready for sea, to be delivered to me on or before the second day of June." Brown accepted the deal, and *America* left New York on June 21, arriving at Le Havre, France, on July 11, 1851. It was there that the yacht was prepared fully for racing—its final coat of paint put on and its racing sails bent on spars replacing those used for delivery—away from the prying eyes of English yachtsmen.

THERE IS NO SECOND

When *America* finally reached British waters later in the summer of 1851, it was anchored a few miles east of Cowes, Isle of Wight. In the morning, *America* was met by the racing cutter *Laverock,* one of the fastest of the Royal Yacht Squadron fleet. Although this was not an official race, it seemed an obvious challenge to the American yacht's performance. *America* beat to windward for those few miles, quickly outpacing the British cutter. The victory marked *America* as a potentially superior vessel, and few, if any, yachtsmen were willing to take up the challenge of racing against it in a match.

PAGE 18: Designed by George Steers and built by R. H. Wilson, the schooner *America* beat seventeen boats in the Royal Yacht Squadron fleet thanks to its hard-driving crew, unprecedented design, and well-cut cotton sails. • BELOW: Map of the Isle of Wight and the 53-mile course of the legendary race held on August 22, 1851, which began and ended at Cowes.

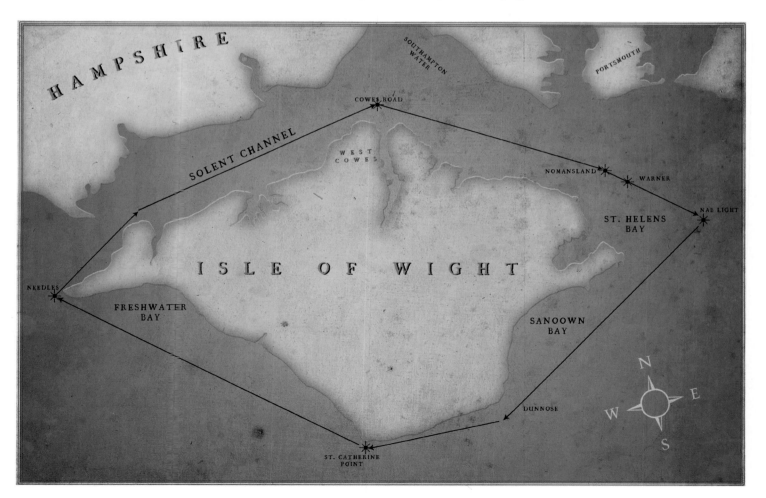

LEFT: Commodore John Cox Stevens receiving Queen Victoria on board *America* after winning the £100 Cup. • INSERT: Poster for the Royal Yacht Squadron races of August 1851.

Even after this display of speed, Stevens and his cohorts made every effort to obtain a match for high stakes—a figure of 10,000 guineas was suggested (equivalent to $3 million today). But they did nothing to enhance their chances when they sailed round with the King's Cup fleet on August 18, starting 3 miles behind and overtaking the entire fleet in an hour and thirty-eight minutes. The following day, Stevens was allowed to enter a RYS regatta on August 22 for the £100 Cup. It was the only event that *America* would sail except for a match against Robert Stephenson's 100-ton schooner, *Titania*, six days later over a 20-mile course from the Nab Light and back for £100. But it was the race against the entire RYS that would prove to be the most significant event in yacht-racing history.

It is, after all, the £100 Cup for the race around the Isle of Wight that *America* is justly famed. Starting behind the fleet from the Royal Yacht Squadron, *America* overtook them before the race was half run and surged away around the back of the Isle of Wight with a substantial lead. After *America* finished at Cowes, the *Times* reported: "Off Cowes were innumerable yachts and on every side was heard the hail is the *America* first? The answer, yes. What is second? The reply—nothing." This almost certainly gave credence to the apocryphal story that Queen Victoria had asked a signalman, on being told that the *America* was first, "Who is second?" The signalman is said to have replied, "Ma'am, there is no second."

EVEN IN VICTORY, there was one minor hiccup: George Ackers, the owner of the three-masted schooner *Brilliant*, protested *America* for sailing inside the Nab Light. But he withdrew the protest when he discovered that the instructions

ROYAL YACHT SQUADRON
REGATTA,
1851.

ON MONDAY, AUGUST 18th,
HER MAJESTY'S CUP,

By Large Class Cutters of the R.Y.S. (105 Tons and above.) If three enter before Midnight, August 1st, if not, it will be open to R.Y.S. Cutters from 50 and under 100 Tons, to close at Midnight, Saturday, August 9th.

TUESDAY, AUGUST 19th,
THE R.Y.S. ANNUAL DINNER.

WEDNESDAY, AUGUST 20th,
HIS ROYAL HIGHNESS
PRINCE ALBERT'S CUP,

By Large Class R.Y.S. Schooners (140 Tons and above.) If three enter before Midnight, August 1st, if not, it will be open to the Small Class R.Y.S. Schooners (under 140 Tons,) to close at Midnight, Saturday, August 9th.

THURSDAY, AUGUST 21st,
THE
R.Y.S. ANNUAL BALL.

+ Subscription ap - By Yachts of any RY Clubs not exceeding 30 Tons. Start at Glen

FRIDAY, AUGUST 22nd,
THE R.Y.S. £100 CUP,

Open to Yachts belonging to the Clubs of all Nations, to close at Midnight, August 16th.
No Time allowed for Tonnage.
Three Vessels must enter and start for each Prize, or no Race.

FIREWORKS
At 9, P.M., August 22nd.

JOHN BATES,
SECRETARY.

issued to the *America* did not contain any directive as to which hand this light vessel should be passed. Such controversies soon would become symptomatic of America's Cup challenges.

The controversy didn't stop there. The Marquess of Anglesey, then eighty years old, had watched *America* sail in Cowes harbor from his own yacht, *Pearl*, with the master of the yacht, who said: "Your Lordship knows that no vessel with sails alone could do that." When Lord Anglesey went aboard *America*, he went straight to the stern and checked whether there was a propeller. On discovering none and seeing that *America*, with its fine bow and beam well aft, was unlike any in the RYS, he remarked, "If she is right, we must all be wrong." This comment has subsequently been repeated by those in search of sailing's Holy Grail—*America* had something that no other boat in the Royal Yacht Squadron had, and it wasn't a propeller.

"Your Lordship knows that no vessel with sails alone could do that."

Although it is painfully obvious that British yachtsmen and the Royal Yacht Squadron denied *America* "high stakes" matches, the syndicate of owners did make a small profit on their investment by selling *America* to Lord John de Blaquiere for £5,000—a value of $25,000 at the time. They returned home without a boat and without great winnings, but left the RYS baffled and short one £100 Cup.

THE DEED OF GIFT

Despite the remarkable victory, the six who had built and campaigned *America* returned to New York to a mild reception. Rather than pockets filled with winnings, they brought only a silver trophy as evidence of their success. For a year at least, the trophy did the rounds of dinner parties, where it was little more than a conversation piece. That the silver cup was destined to become the oldest trophy in modern sports and sailing's most coveted prize would have seemed absurd, and its allure might have been lost entirely if not for the international beckon established by the Deed of Gift.

Those who had won the cup wished it to be held in high esteem and presented it to the New York Yacht Club as a trophy for an international match to be sailed for by "yachts of any foreign country . . . it is to be distinctly understood that the Cup is to be the property of the Club and not of the members thereof, or owners of the vessel winning it in the match, and that the conditions of keeping it open to be sailed for by Yacht Clubs of all foreign countries shall forever attach to it, thus making it perpetually a Challenge Cup for friendly competition between foreign countries." The cup had been won in international competition, and those responsible for the win wanted to inspire high-level international match racing. The Deed of Gift did just that, effectively launching the competition known as the America's Cup.

THE DEED OF GIFT was dated July 8, 1857, and less than two weeks later, the NYYC attempted to initiate possible challengers by sending a notice to a group of foreign yacht clubs.

Partly because of the Civil War, thirteen years would pass before a challenge was made. When it finally came, in 1870, the challenger, Englishman James Ashbury, a rich industrialist born the son of a wheelwright who invented the railway carriage, was met not by one boat in a match as the deed had indicated but by the entire NYYC fleet of fifteen boats. At the time, this was seen as a payback for the Royal Yacht Squadron failing to give *America* a match. Ashbury's boat, *Cambria*, was eighth to finish and tenth on corrected time. Although Ashbury was unsuccessful in his challenge—the first for the America's Cup—he won the hearts of a public that had taken an unexpected interest in the event.

Undeterred by defeat, Ashbury returned the following year with his new yacht, *Livonia*, and began a series of arguments over the outcome of the racing. On October 16, 1871, *Livonia* lost the first of four races to Franklin Osgood's *Columbia*. In the next race, two days later, Ashbury led around the outer mark of a leeward/windward course and took the outer mark to starboard, gybing in the process. *Columbia* left the mark to port, tacking around in a much safer and simpler maneuver, but Ashbury believed that the American yacht's move was incorrect, as he had not received the instruction issued to *Columbia* that the outer mark could be taken on either hand. He made the score of race wins 1–1, while the NYYC maintained a score of 2–0.

Livonia won the third race in a strong breeze. When *Columbia* was replaced as the defending yacht by William Douglass's *Sappho* for the fourth race, Ashbury was again unhappy (his idea of a match was against a single named boat), particularly when he was beaten by more than half an hour. *Sappho* did much the same in the fifth race to take the America's Cup by 4–1, but Ashbury

> "Mr. Ashbury seems to look behind every action for an unworthy motive, and seek in every explanation evidences of concealment and want of candor."
>
> —NYYC IN A LETTER ADDRESSED TO THE ROYAL YACHT SQUADRON

> "The Americans were too cute to conduct races on the moral level that existed in England."
>
> —JAMES ASHBURY

ABOVE: *Mischief* and *Atalanta* in the first race of Canada's second challenge for the America's Cup. • OPPOSITE: *Sappho* replaced *Columbia* to defeat Ashbury's *Livonia*. Here *Sappho* navigates among spectacular boats during the pennultimate race of the 1871 America's Cup.

claimed that he had won the second race and that the score was only 3–2 in the defender's favor. He announced to the New York Yacht Club that he would sail the next race the following day, whether or not there was another yacht to meet him, and that he would sail over the course the same way. By Ashbury's count, he defeated the NYYC 3–4. The America's Cup, however, with the official score 4–1, remained the property of the club. Winning the £100 Cup in 1851 might have been remarkable, but defending the America's Cup was quickly becoming an obsession, and taking it back wouldn't be easy.

The next two challenges for the America's Cup came from Canada. The first, in 1876, was from Charles Gifford, the vice commodore of the Royal Canadian Yacht Club, whose schooner, *Countess of Dufferin*, was met by a similarly sized schooner, *Madeleine*, and beaten comfortably in the two races. On the second day, *America*, designed twenty-five years earlier, sailed the same course twenty minutes quicker than the *Countess of Dufferin*.

The second came from Captain Alexander Cuthbert, a Scottish-born "chancer," always ready for a gamble, who mounted the next challenge with the yacht *Atalanta* from Canada's Bay of Quinte Yacht Club. *Atalanta* was late in build, and Cuthbert decided to use the Erie Canal to transport it to New York for completion, towing the boat on its side with a team of mules. *Atalanta's*

THIS PAGE: Port quarter view of cutter *Valkyrie II* under sail. Designed by George L. Watson and built by D&W Henderson & Co., the boat was beaten by *Vigilant* in the 1893 America's Cup. • OPPOSITE: The 123-foot cutter *Defender*, built and designed by Nat Herreshoff 1895, was the subject of much controversy but ultimately defeated Dunraven's *Valkyrie III*.

"To-day, on the reach home, eight cr nine steamers crossed my bow, several were to windward of me, and, what was worse, a block of steamers were steaming level with me, and close under my lee . . . To race under those conditions is in my opinion, absurd."

—LORD DUNRAVEN IN A LETTER TO THE CUP COMMITTEE, SEPTEMBER 10, 1895

Dunraven was convinced that considerable reballasting of *Defender* was taking place during the regatta.

The overenthusiastic spectators in a larger-than-ever fleet of streamers were also providing problems for Dunraven, crowding close to *Valkyrie III* most of the time, and he raised serious complaints to the NYYC committee. Finally, when he received no satisfaction, he took *Valkyrie III* to the start of the final race, crossed the start line, and returned to harbor, allowing *Defender* to sail the course unchallenged.

On his return to England, Dunraven, in a letter published in the *Field*, complained of what he considered the irregular behavior of the defender, making allegations related to illegal reballasting and complaints about the crowding of the course. The NYYC decided to investigate his complaints and called Dunraven to New York at the end of December 1895. The balance of evidence presented was in favor of the defending club, which found that there was no justification for the complaints. Dunraven eschewed international yacht racing for the rest of his life.

The unpleasantness around the controversy marked the end of the "friendly" era and put a stop to America's Cup racing for four years. The competition needed a challenger prepared to accept what had taken place as merely a temporary glitch in an otherwise outstanding sporting contest. It needed the good-humored, enterprising grocer from Glasgow, Sir Thomas Lipton. ◄

Lipton was the first to use his America's Cup challenges for commercial gain and promotion. A century later, commercial sponsorship would be commonplace. The roots of this sponsorship stem from the enterprising characters that populated the event's early history. Initially, rich men attempted to promote their own causes through association with the America's Cup and to develop financial liaisons. Appreciating this, Lipton realized there was much to gain, even in losing.

His uses of the America's Cup challenges were such that newspapers printed stories describing his rise from his early days as a dock laborer in New York, his American businesses that included pork-packing interests in the West, and his vast tea plantations in Ceylon (Sri Lanka). These articles also detailed his graciousness as a host at dinner parties and his chivalry toward American women. He was voted the most democratic man ever to challenge for the America's Cup and a gracious loser—all very good for his business and his persona.

BELOW: Herreshoff cutters *Constitution,* in the lead, and *Columbia,* racing in an early Cup trial in 1901.

A FORESHADOW OF THE 34ᵀᴴ AMERICA'S CUP

Despite Sir Thomas Lipton's constant defeats, Lipton's tea sales in the United States soared with every challenge. This led others to believe there were opportunities in hosting the America's Cup. On the West Coast, the California Promotion Committee had the idea of staging the next races off San Francisco. In 1903, the committee sent a letter to C. Oliver Iselin, the managing partner of *Reliance*, suggesting that it could offer near perfect conditions in San Francisco Bay, with regular winds from June to August in the landlocked harbor. The New York Yacht Club was the holder of the America's Cup, and it would have been unthinkable for the club to schedule racing anywhere but at its own regatta site. More than a century went by before a San Francisco club would win the America's Cup and make the dream of hosting the event amid such ideal conditions a reality.

INSERT: A 1903 telegram from the California Promotion Committee inviting the New York Yacht Club to host the America's Cup in San Francisco Bay.

PERSISTENCE WAS the keynote of Lipton's challenges—there were five, all unsuccessful, but he never became an embittered loser. Immediately after the first *Shamrock* was defeated by J. P. Morgan's *Columbia* in 1899, Lipton lodged another challenge through the Royal Ulster Yacht Club with *Shamrock II* for 1901. Again, he was beat by *Columbia*—the first boat to successfully defend the trophy twice—but was not deterred.

During the defender trials of Lipton's second challenge, another entrepreneur attempted to use the America's Cup for promotion. Seeing the growing public appeal, Thomas W. Lawson (later noted for his book *History of the America's Cup*) attempted to break into the event. He held that it was the right of every American to take part in the defense but was rejected by the NYYC because he refused to join the club. His *Independence* was finally chartered to a member and entered in the trials, without success. *Independence* did, however, point the way for fifty-five-year-old Nat to develop his fifth America's Cup design for the 1903 defense, *Reliance*. Once again, Lipton would be the challenger.

OPPOSITE: Launch of the Herreshoff-designed *Reliance*. At 144 feet, *Reliance* was the largest single-masted racing sailboat ever built. • ABOVE: Known as the "Wizard of Bristol," Nat Herreshoff designed five America's Cup defenders between 1893 and 1920. • PAGE 42: Sir Thomas Lipton inspecting the hull of his 110-foot cutter *Shamrock IV* while it was hauled out at Morse Dry Dock, Island City, New York in 1920. • PAGE 43: The 106-foot Herreshoff cutter *Resolute* to the lee of the 110-foot cutter *Shamrock IV* at the start of the fifth race of the 1920 America's Cup.

Herreshoff's creation was the largest single-hull yacht ever to compete for the America's Cup. It was a magnificent display of the boats prior to the J-Class era—enormous, beautiful, lavish, and fast—and a clear response to Lipton's impressive, if unsuccessful, *Shamrocks*. *Reliance* was 202 feet (almost as long as Boeing 747) from the tip of its bowsprit to the end of its overhanging boom, more than double its hull waterline of 89 feet 8 inches. In displacement yachts—the order of the day in the early 1900s—speed was related directly to waterline length and the power available from the sails: The longer the waterline and the greater the sail area, the faster the boat. This simple formula, however, comes with an escalation of disproportionate costs on an almost exponential basis. *Reliance* carried 19,169 square feet of sail and was manned by a crew of sixty-four. The spectacular boat defeated Lipton's *Shamrock III* comfortably. Even in defeat, Lipton's tea sales in the United States soared. Although he hadn't won the America's Cup, he was certainly winning at his own game.

DESPITE HIS FINANCIAL SUCCESS and perhaps, in part, because of his several losses, Lipton was bold enough to suggest changes to the size of boat used for the America's Cup in order to stop budgets from spiraling out of control. In 1907, he wrote to the NYYC suggesting a series of races to be sailed in 1908 in yachts of 75-foot waterline. Incidentally, a year earlier, the admiral of the Royal Swedish Yacht Club had asked the club whether it was open to receive a challenge in 1909 in boats of 70-foot waterline. This clearly suggested that Lipton was generating a broader interest in winning the America's Cup, should challenging become affordable.

After the NYYC America's Cup Committee fully discussed Lipton's suggestion, Commodore Ledyard proposed, and Commodore J. P. Morgan seconded, a resolution declaring that the America's Cup was "a trophy which stands pre-eminently for speed and for the utmost skill in designing, construction, managing, and handling the competing vessels, and should, therefore, be sailed for by the fastest and most powerful vessels that can be produced." The resolution added, "The importance of the event makes it desirable that the contesting vessel should be substantially of the greatest power and size permitted by the limitations of the Deed of Gift."

"a trophy which stands pre-eminently for speed and for the utmost skill in designing, construction, managing, and handling the competing vessels, and should, therefore, be sailed for by the fastest and most powerful vessels that can be produced."

There was much criticism of the NYYC's decision to reject Lipton's challenge. In the October *Yachtsman*, the editor stated, "There is no yachtsman in Europe that would dare risk the lives of a large crew in a flimsy craft which the New York Yacht Club now insists on for the cup races. The whole structure must be built in the lightest possible manner. What chance, then, has a

European yacht of this type against one built in America?" An editorial in the *World* added, "Truly the cup is now safe."

But Lipton was both persuasive and charismatic, and in the autumn of 1912, he approached the NYYC in person in an effort to persuade the club to amend the conditions of the rules governing America's Cup races. "I have a feeling," he said, "that they will meet me. If they don't, they might as well bury the cup. At present the rules permit a freak to race for the cup and it is impossible to build a freak, which has a chance of winning and has to cross the Atlantic." Somewhat characteristically, he stated that if the club agreed to alter the conditions so that he had a chance, he would build two yachts to the plans of the best designers in Britain. He pointed out that the Universal Rules under which he challenged were American rules and that yachts built to them must cross the ocean.

Finally, the NYYC agreed to a challenge from the Royal Ulster Yacht Club with a yacht of 75-foot waterline, made on July 29, 1913, for a match the following year. It had taken seven years of almost continuous negotiation to find agreement with the NYYC. Lipton's persistence may not have wrested the trophy, but it certainly kept it within reach.

Then World War I intervened. Lipton's *Shamrock IV* paused at the Azores during its transatlantic crossing and continued on July 29, 1914, the day after Austria-Hungary declared war with Serbia and a month after the assassination of Archduke Franz Ferdinand at Sarajevo. *Shamrock IV* was 1,000 miles from Bermuda when it received radio instructions to alter course to the island because of the danger from patrolling German raiders following Britain's declaration of war on August 4. The next day day, Lipton withdrew his challenge for 1914.

Shamrock IV finally reached New York on August 16 and was laid up until the armistice was declared in November 11, 1918. A month later, Lipton reopened his challenge for a contest in 1919. The NYYC declined this challenge, stating that 1920 was a more appropriate time, and to this Lipton eventually acceded. The challenge would prove to be Lipton's best attempt at taking the America's Cup from the NYYC.

Despite giving the Henry Walters defender, *Resolute*, seven minutes on handicap, *Shamrock IV* led by 2–0, and Lipton's delight was unabashed.

Unfortunately for Lipton and his many public supporters, *Shamrock IV* lost the next three races, and the trophy remained in the NYYC. Lipton said of his defeat:

> When the *Resolute* recorded the first of her three victories, the margin by which she won was no more than the time my ship had to allow her under the then existing measurement rule. So far as pure sailing was concerned, it was virtually a dead heat. And in one at least of the defender's two other victories rather baffling weather seemed to kike us less that it did our opponent. But I did not grumble. It is all in the game. We had had a series of splendid races, and I had, at any rate, the melancholy satisfaction of knowing that in the final result the better boat had won.

LIPTON WAS UNDETERRED, but not until May 1929 did he issue his fifth challenge. This was to be under the J-Class of the Universal Rule, boats of the size that Lipton had favored a quarter of a century earlier. Despite the economic situation, four defense candidates were built, the best of which proved to be *Enterprise* skippered by Harold S. "Mike" Vanderbilt. *Enterprise* was undeniably faster than *Shamrock V*, mainly because it had been more effectively tuned in the trials and races earlier in the season and had defeated the challenger 4–0.

With his 23-Meter Class *Shamrock* and his large steam yacht, *Erin*, from which he watched the regatta, Lipton's final challenge was a display of wealth. It was matched, however, by those who commissioned the four J-Class yachts that campaigned to defend the Cup, and throughout the 1930s, this remained the pattern, with little commercial reward. The two challenges from aviation pioneer Sir T. O. M. Sopwith in 1934 and 1937 were of a purely sporting nature. In the design and rigging of his yachts, *Endeavour* and *Endeavour II*, Sopwith employed the technology that made his aircraft world leaders, but both lost to Vanderbilt's *Rainbow* and *Ranger*. ◄

LEFT: Workers build the mast of Harold Vanderbilt's *Rainbow* at the Herreshoff Manufacturing Company using rivets and what were technologically advanced materials at the time   ABOVE: Spectator vessels, including the 304-foot steam yacht *Corsair*, line up for the second race of the 1920 America's Cup between *Shamrock IV* and the defender *Resolute*. • PAGES 46–47: J-Class yachts undersail during the New York Yacht Club Cruise on Buzzard's Bay. Shown is *Ranger* in the foreground, followed by *Rainbow*, *Endeavour*, *Endeavour II*, and *Yankee*. Together, these boats represent the beginning and end of the J-Class era.

3

PERPETUAL
CHALLENGES

MARK CHISNELL

The factors that make up the drama of the America's Cup are several, but it's the boats that are the centerpieces of every competition. Contests for the America's Cup tend to be remembered for one of two reasons: because they were particularly close or, more often, because of the dominance of the victor.

Sometimes that dominance was due to the woeful ineptitude of the loser. On other occasions, it was because the winner was a breakthrough boat, a technological marvel of its time. Such was the case with *America*, whose cotton sails and radical sharp-bowed shape changed the course of yacht design and upset Britain's self-styled rule over the waves. The boat may have been built to win wagers, but ultimately it inspired a battle for status in maritime engineering prowess that has defined the America's Cup ever since.

The boat may have been built to win wagers, but ultimately it inspired a battle for status in maritime engineering prowess that has defined the America's Cup ever since.

After *America*, the 1903 Nat Herreshoff–designed *Reliance* was the next of these breakthrough boats, sporting ball-bearing and auto-shifting winches that would still look cutting edge in concept half a century later. It was followed at the end of the J-Class era by *Ranger*, among whose innovations was the first synthetic sail. It was a radical-looking boat, and the designers thought it was a little too radical to be built, but some remarkable tank-testing results gave them the confidence to go forward.

On this occasion, the process of testing the performance of scale models—by towing them up and down a huge tank of water—turned out to be an

accurate predictor of full-size speed, although subsequently the limitations of the method would be revealed. *Ranger*'s utter dominance was the last of the J-Class era, for although the Great Depression had barely dented the attraction of these extraordinary craft for a certain type of wealthy man, World War II was to have a more serious effect. A change in the Deed of Gift was necessary to revive the America's Cup amid the postwar austerity, and in 1956, the minimum waterline length was reduced to 44 feet, making possible the 1958 Royal Yacht Squadron challenge in 12-Meters. At around 45 feet, these were significantly smaller boats in contrast to a J-Class's waterline length of around 75 feet. The 12-Meter was correspondingly cheaper. Still, innovation and engineering remained paramount to success.

The 12-Meter was designed to the International or Meter Rule. First formulated in 1907, it had subsequently become the core of European and Olympic yacht racing. It worked by taking a series of measurements of hull, mast, and sails, then inputting the numbers into an equation:

Rating = $(L + 2d - F + \sqrt{S}) / 2.37$

L = length (meters)

d = girth difference (meters)

F = freeboard (meters)

S = sail area (square meters)

The equation's answer defined the type of International Rule boat. For the 12-Meter, the measurements taken had to produce an answer of 12 or less. In this way, the key speed-generating parameters like waterline length and sail area could be balanced and offset against each other. If designers wanted more power, they could perhaps add more sail area, but they would also have to do something to slow the boat down—like shorten its length—to keep the result of the equation at 12 meters.

The introduction of this popular racing class to the America's Cup revived competition, and challenges followed at a brisk clip in 1962, 1964, and 1967. Although the switch may have made the America's Cup viable again, and initially more accessible, the intensity of the competition was quickly and inevitably upping the ante. There was another breakthrough boat in 1967, with Olin Stephens'—designed *Intrepid*. The boat was the product of a full year of tank testing and was innovative in several areas. The keel was smaller, with the rudder separated from it and put much farther aft. It used a flap, or trim tab, for the first time in the America's Cup, and skipper Bus Mosbacher put all the winches belowdecks, where seven of the twelve crew would spend the race. *Intrepid* was as fast as it was original and won four straight races against Australia's *Dame Pattie*.

Just in case anyone had forgotten, *Intrepid*'s innovations made the primacy of the engineering and design battle clear. But there was no shortage of takers for this perpetual trial of intellect, and by 1970 there were four putative challengers, of which two showed up, France and Australia. For the first time, two nations

OPPOSITE, TOP: Emil "Bus" Mosbacher Jr. at the helm of the Britton Chance Jr.–designed *Intrepid* before 12-Meter class trials in June, 1967. • OPPOSITE, BOTTOM: American defender *Weatherly* leading Australian 12-Meter sloop *Gretel* in the fourth race of the 1962 America's Cup.

ABOVE, LEFT: Ted Turner and his defender, *Courageous*, would spoil yet another Austrailian challenge in 1977. • ABOVE, RIGHT: Australia's *Southern Cross* in the boatlift. *Southern Cross* couldn't defeat Dennis Conner and *Courageous* in 1974, but it was the first campaign headed by Alan Bond, who, with John Bertrand, would eventually take the America's Cup to Australia.

faced off to find a challenger, and *Gretel II* won for Australia. It went on to meet *Intrepid*, whose legend was reinforced by becoming one of only three two-time defenders, and then beating the Australians 4–1. The score, however, belied the speed of the loser; it seemed that the introduction of competition among the challengers was improving their performance in the technology game.

In 1974, France and Australia once again turned up to race for the right to challenge the New York Yacht Club. This time the Australian challenger was funded by Alan Bond, an English-born sign writer who had built a substantial property empire in Western Australia. The designer of Bond's *Southern Cross* was Bob Miller (who later called himself Ben Lexcen), and they lost 4–0 to *Courageous*. *Courageous* was another Stephens two-time defender, one that would influence the design of 12-Meters until the end of their Cup era. The boat's starting helmsman and tactician was Dennis Conner, and it turned out that this was the opening round in a long battle between Bond, Lexcen, Conner, and their cohorts that would eventually change the America's Cup forever.

The record shows that in 1977, *Courageous*, this time steered by Ted Turner (the same man who started CNN and married Jane Fonda), beat Alan Bond's second challenger (called *Australia* but also designed by Lexcen) by a resounding four straight races. Turner famously slumped into his chair at the press conference after some serious celebrating on the way back to the dock. Apart from that, what went on in the background was in many ways more interesting. The technology battle had ramped up the game to another level.

On the challengers' side, the Swedish had brought *Sverige*, with innovations like tiller steering and leg-powered winches. In the end, these turned out to be novelties, but the challengers were trying. The defense trials had a much more lasting impact, fought out between boats run by the principals of the great U.S. sailmaking businesses, Lowell North and Ted Hood. After the high-profile failure of Britton Chance Jr.'s *Mariner,* the previous Cup had demonstrated that the

NOT YACHTIES, ATHLETES

The changes in boats and technology have dramatically altered the demands on sailors since the J-Class era in the 1930s. Before the J-Class, almost everything was done by hand, with minimum help from winches and pulley systems. Racing the J-Class boats was both physically demanding and dangerous, and several men were lost overboard. But the crews were professional seamen, often hard-as-nails fishermen used to hauling nets in winter storms and to the loss of friends and shipmates.

The 12-Meter era changed all that. Not only were the boats smaller and less powerful, but initially they carried a largely amateur crew. Still, there were a lot fewer of them, only twelve men on board, and they needed to be fit, as the boats were demanding when they were being maneuvered. The toughest of the 12-Meter Cups was in 1987, when the Indian Ocean off Western Australia provided the waves, and the heat of the interior a consistently strong breeze. Crewmen got used to sailing with bruised and sore bodies and cuts that wouldn't heal under the perpetual dousing from salt water.

ABOVE: Grinders hard at work cranking on a genoa sheet winch or "coffee gringer," onboard *Weatherly*. The small crews of the 12-Meters demanded strength and agility, something the AC72s, with their extreme power and eleven-man crews, take to an unprecedented level.

These were now mainly professional racing sailors, selected and trained for the physical and mental requirements of their job. Strong, agile men up the front wrestled the sails up and down, and big powerful men in the middle of the boat, with the aerobic capacity of Olympic rowers, turned the winches and pulled in the sails. At the back, the job was less about the body and more about the mind.

The coming of the International America's Cup Class meant more powerful boats, but help was at hand for the crews. The venues of San Diego, Auckland, and Valencia were nothing like as tough as Western Australia had been, with generally lighter wind and flatter water. And technology helped out with new materials, more efficient winch systems, and lighter ropes and gear. The intellectual demands were also changing, as computers delivered more information and data, and the decision-making process became more sophisticated. The 2010 America's Cup was unique in that the boats had engines installed for power winches, and the two fragile multihulls went in straight lines as much as they could. All the crews from the very beginning had been

fortunate in that respect; the racing was often a speed test with only limited maneuvers. This was an intellectual game, played by the helmsman and his team of sail trimmers and tacticians. It gave the guys at the front of the boat the time for a breather.

The racecourse in San Francisco for 2013 ends that, compressing the racing into a smaller area than ever before and combining it with the fastest boats ever seen in the Cup. The athletic demands of the 34th America's Cup go beyond all that had gone before. As Kevin Hall, a member of Artemis Racing for the 2013 Cup and previously the navigator for the Emirates Team New Zealand boat in the 2007 America's Cup, put it, "It feels like the last two minutes of a basketball game that has had no subs, with the court bucking under your feet, everyone on the other team taller than you, and sometimes even the fans themselves are between you and the hoop. If that wasn't enough, the correct strategy can change instantly with the huge difference between a good and bad acceleration after a maneuver. The real challenge is thinking clearly all day in this scenario with such a high heart rate."

ABOVE: Emirates Team New Zealand's AC72 is designed to have up to eight crew members grinding the same winch.

tank-testing results weren't always accurate. Hood and North had realized the limitations and changed the way they went about their preparation for the defense trials. Instead of spending development time and money in the tank, they built earlier and went sailing, and in doing so they opened a completely new front in the technology war. Speed testing full-size yachts had its own set of instrumentation and measurement issues, and multiplied the opportunities for the development of new equipment across the hull, foils, sails, masts, and deck gear.

TOP: *Intrepid* (US-22) and *Courageous* under sail during the 1974 America's Cup trials. • BOTTOM: Halsey Herreshoff, grandson of Nat Herreshoff, fulfilling his role as navigator for the American defender *Freedom* in the 1980 America's Cup.

Ted Hood's *Independence*, launched a year early, sailed against Turner and *Courageous* until the Marblehead, Massachusetts, harbor froze. Meanwhile, Lowell North launched *Enterprise* and started working it up in the West Coast's winter sunshine against *Intrepid*. But both Hood and North seemed to get too wrapped up in the technical and commercial contest and ignored the boat racing. This allowed Turner to come through on the outside and win the defender berth. Nevertheless, the idea of building boats much earlier and spending the time sailing and training stuck.

All but one of the seven contenders for the 1980 America's Cup were built early, and long campaigns of boat tuning and modifying were now the accepted norm. This approach had a lot of consequences, not least that the full-time teams needed a new kind of sailor, as Halsey Herreshoff (Conner's navigtor and grandson of the designer Nat Herreshoff) put it: "The days when a New York stockbroker will leave his business for a month or two and race in the America's Cup are over." Now the boats were sailed by industry professionals, sailmakers and riggers, or just flat-out professional sailors.

THE PROFESSIONAL ERA

Alan Bond, with a pimped-up *Australia*, won the right to challenge in 1980, and he faced Dennis Conner in *Freedom*, an Olin Stephens design. Conner had destroyed his American opposition for the defender's berth and then put

"The days when a New York stockbroker will leave his business for a month or two and race in the America's Cup are over."

BELOW: *Freedom* and *Australia* crossing during the 1980 America's Cup. *Australia* lost but the Aussies would return three years later to wrest the America's Cup from the New York Yacht Club.

Australia away 4–1. This achievement was on the back of a reported 150 days of sailing, testing a hundred different sails, and Conner did it despite the Aussie's late introduction of an innovation copied from the British boat *Lionheart*. This was a bendy topmast that increased sail area and made the sails very fast in

> "It [sailing] basically was an art before. We're just starting to scratch it into a science."
>
> —DENNIS CONNER

light air. Two lessons could be taken away from the series. First, the possibility of game-changing engineering and design innovation was still very much alive; second, no one could spend enough time and money out on the water.

Over the next three years, the search for speed expanded exponentially, as anyone who could raise the money adopted Conner's modus operandi. Five countries and seven boats would race for the right to challenge in 1983, in what was to be called the Louis Vuitton Cup. Conner would build three new boats (in addition to modifying *Freedom*) in his quest to defend. Bobbing along in this tidal wave of time and money was the computer, first used aboard *Intrepid* in 1967, but which now found applications in every area, like sail design in the new materials of Kevlar and Mylar. The silicon chip had even started to appear on the boats, a previously unimaginable notion.

The teams that finally squared up for the 1983 America's Cup match were Dennis Conner's *Liberty* and Alan Bond's *Australia II*. The former was the product of Conner's formidable four-boat development program and the countless hours of testing. *Australia II* had a leaner background, training against a second Australian boat, called *Challenge 12*, that was also designed by Lexcen but was operated by a separate team. However, *Australia II* had a keel like no other 12-Meter. Lexcen had taken a leaf from *Lionheart*'s book of innovation, gone back to tank testing, and then designed a boat that was to irrevocably change the course of the America's Cup, and begin the modern era of professional sailboat racing. But it would still take a consummate sporting performance to pry the trophy from American hands. ◄

LEFT: *Defender* (US-33) and *Liberty* covering each other before the start of 1983 America's Cup race. *Defender* acted as a trial horse for Dennis Conner's *Liberty* leading up to the 1983 America's Cup. • BELOW: 1980 America's Cup defender *Freedom* skippered by Dennis Conner.

4

MAKING WAY
FOR MULTIPLE
CHALLENGERS

➤ KIMBALL LIVINGTON ◄

I t's worn-out cornball to call the America's Cup the Holy Grail of yachting. And yet, for 132 years, taking the America's Cup away from the United States seemed as farfetched and unachievable as uncovering that magic chalice. That is probably why, in 1970, not one but four would-be challengers appeared. Everest too was unachievable, until it wasn't.

The New York Yacht Club was not obligated to accommodate four challengers and a growing international interest. The club's obligation under the Deed of Gift was to defend the trophy against a legitimate foreign challenger. In doing so in the past, it had often been pilloried—sometimes correctly, sometimes not—for stacking the deck in its favor. A bit more criticism now for guarding the castle surely couldn't have hurt. But the Americans chose instead to embrace a new day and let the event grow. Fully aware that in the long run this would strengthen the opposition, NYYC's defense committee agreed to allow would-be challengers to conduct their own trials series, with the understanding that the best of them, the winner, would be accepted as the challenger for the 1970 America's Cup.

By custom, the Americans relied on a committee of NYYC's elder statesmen, the "Straw Hats" as they were called, after their headgear, who would spend the summer watching the American hopefuls race. These gentlemen would even halt and restart a race, like puppet masters, if they felt like it. Eventually, in their wisdom, they would "excuse" contenders until a boat and a skipper was chosen. The subjective element was tempered by the certainty that they were not going to pick a slower boat.

The 1970 America's Cup match was agreed to be a best-of-seven race series, which the challengers agreed to mimic in their selection trials. Sir Frank Packer, in his second attempt on behalf of Australia, produced the Alan Payne–designed *Gretel II*. Like its 1962 predecessor, *Gretel II* was fast and capable of taking the America's Cup—if the stars aligned in favor of the Aussies, and if ever they could match the sailing mastery of the Americans. Baron Marcel Bich, demonstrating

"An Australian skipper protesting to the New York Yacht Club Committee is like a man complaining to his mother-in-law about his wife."

—SIR FRANCIS PACKER

PAGES 60-61: *Stars & Stripes* on the right, and New Zealand's *KZ7*, left, off the famously rough waters of Fremantle, Australia, during the 1987 Louis Vuitton Cup. • OPPOSITE, TOP: The "Straw Hats" enroute to dismissing the defender hopeful *Courageous* and to inform Dennis Conner and the *Liberty* crew that they had been chosen to defend for the 1983 America's Cup. • OPPOSITE, BOTTOM: Baron Marcel Bich in 1969. By bringing on Bruno Troublé as his skipper, Bich would indirectly have a hand in founding the Louis Vuitton Cup.

the financial clout of the ubiquitous Bic pen, came to town with a collection of veteran 12-Meters, a wine cellar, two chefs, and a challenger, *France*, that had been designed in-country on the "inspiration" of yet another 12-Meter, commissioned for the purpose by Bich from American designer Britton Chance Jr.

Baron Bich was not a sailor but a successful gentleman who relished challenge. When someone told him in 1965 that there was an event that was impossible to win, he lifted an eyebrow and listened, "It is impossible? I will go after it!" Immediately, he bought *Sovereign* and *Constellation* and started sailing with a huge team in France.

It was Bich who first advocated for the idea of a challenger selection process, and during the 1967 match the New York Yacht Club announced it's intention to accept the Baron's idea of multiple challengers for the 1970 match.

With his stable of boats and his entourage, Bich cut quite a figure in Newport, but the Aussies in the trials simply handed him his tail. Bich fired first one skipper, then another, and took the helm himself for the final race. Resplendent in a tailored white suit and white gloves, he proceeded to become lost in a fogbank that engulfed the racecourse, and he came ashore roundly criticizing the Race Committee. Bich, however, allowed Packer's team to use *France* as a trial horse. France thus helped the challenger gauge modifications to *Gretel II* that continued right up to race time and their first meeting with the defender, *Intrepid*. This was a great help to the challenger, and by returning for future attempts, bringing Olympian and small-boat champion Bruno Troublé as his skipper, Bich would indirectly make his mark on history.

LEFT: *Canada 1* was one of seven 12-Meters that vied for the opportunity to challenge the Americans in 1983. It was Canada's first foray in the America's Cup since the country's embarrassing Deed-of-Gift-changing challenge in 1881. • ABOVE: *France 3*, originally owned by Baron Bich, and helmed here by Bruno Troublé, used *Canada 1* as a sparring partner throughout the lead-up to the 1983 Louis Vuitton Cup.

FOUNDING THE LOUIS VUITTON CUP

Bich's new skipper was more than just a boat driver. As a lad of seventeen, Bruno Troublé had toured the model room of the New York Yacht Club. There, surrounded by the extravagant architecture of the Gilded Age, pacing the rows of models that trace the evolution of the sport of yachting just as surely as they trace the evolution of the America's Cup, he had been dazzled by the history, the romance, the obsessions of one generation after another for the divine

Voilà! La Coupe Louis Vuitton est née.
The Louis Vuitton Cup was born.

madness that is the America's Cup. Now at the helm of an authentic challenger, and schooled in both law and public relations, Troublé recognized an opportunity to recast the challenger series as an event unto itself. A curtain had been opened upon a great stage. Troublé approached Louis Vuitton and made his case for the America's Cup competition as an ideal setting for a luxury goods maker. *Voilà! La Coupe Louis Vuitton est née.* The Louis Vuitton Cup was born.

ABOVE: *Challenge 12*, designed by Ben Lexen, was one of three Australian challengers in 1983. • OPPOSITE, TOP: Dennis Conner (at wheel) and Tom Whidden on *Liberty*, which was ultimately chosen to defend over the other American hopefuls *Magic*, *Spirit of America*, *Courageous*, and Tom Blackaller's *Defender*. • OPPOSITE, BOTTOM: Peter de Savary had high hopes for *Victory '83*, claiming it would be "the best of the Twelves [12-Meters]," but the boat failed to beat what was ultimately an unstoppable *Australia II*.

LOOKING BACK ON THOSE TIMES, Troublé writes, "The America's Cup is a witness to more than one hundred and fifty years of geopolitical change in the Western world, and to the emergence of the Pacific arena as a vital power. Faced with these young, brash bankers of New York, products of a British Empire, who defied—and triumphed over—the era's world masters in 1851; with Australia's triumphing over the West in 1983; with the upstart New Zealanders in 1995, history has stammered. . . ."

In 2013, no guardian of the America's Cup tradition is more stalwart than Bruno Troublé. There is some irony in this, because the very first Louis Vuitton Cup was held in 1983, when the United States' 132-year winning streak came to an end. By that time, the challenger trials had grown to a summer-long knockout, offering both advantages and disadvantages to the eventual challenger. More than once in the years preceding, a challenger had come to town with a boat deliberately biased toward good performance in very light winds. Theory had it that the defender's long summer selection process necessarily produced an all-around performer, but there might eventually be an America's Cup match with enough light-air days to give a light-air flier an edge. As the challenger trials expanded, covering more time and more varied conditions, it became harder to put that theory into practice, but *Australia II* in 1983 was so fast that nothing else mattered.

●——————●——————●

and quality
on last
let by me.
) marked with
blue stripe
the letters
on both ends.
I would like
send early

Yours Truly
Vanderbilt
Loudoun
12
Wednesday

AUSTRALIA II WAS SPECIAL ON MANY COUNTS. The boat was light and carried more sail than its competitors, with a short waterline that made it faster through maneuvers than the competition. But it was the keel, the winged keel as it was called, that turned the trick. The winged keel came as no real surprise to the American defenders. In the spring of 1983, San Francisco's Star Class world champion Tom Blackaller, soon to be skippering a would-be defender named *Defender*, told a gathering at San Francisco's St. Francis Yacht Club that "the Australians have a boat with wings on the keel, or something like that." There was a round of laughter. Four months later, nobody was laughing but the Aussies.

"the Australians have a boat with wings on the keel, or something like that."

OPPOSITE, TOP: Tom Blackaller, San Francisco's native son, was a serious contender in the 1983 defense campaign and an early proponent of an America's Cup in catamarans on San Francisco Bay. "Two of these big cats racing together with the pedal to the metal, flying hulls with the big sails up could be extremely exciting," Blackaller said in 1989. "I'd be back in the America's Cup in a minute if it were held in big, fast boats on San Francisco Bay." • OPPOSITE, BOTTOM: Ben Lexen admiring the radical, winning winged-keel design that helped wrest the trophy from American hands. • ABOVE: From left: *Australia II*, *Canada 1*, Italy's *Azzurra*, and *France 3*. Notice *Australia II*'s skirted keel, a true secret weapon. • INSERT: Letter from Cornelius Vanderbilt to Louis Vuitton requesting a trunk for ocean travel. With the Vanderbilt's involvement in the America's Cup, the letter is the earliest tie to Louis Vuitton's involvement in the event, and a sign of the now famous partnership.

There was ample controversy. The American defenders questioned the legality of the keel, but the momentum was against them. The American defenders had four boats sailing in their trials, but here, too, the momentum was against them. Nothing they had done with new boats, or tweaks to old boats, had produced a 12-Meter that was meaningfully faster than the boat they had sailed three years before, when Dennis Durgan at the side of Dennis Conner called the gambles on the windshifts. This time, as Conner and his new tactician, sailmaker Tom Whidden, took *Liberty* to the line for race one, they had every expectation of being forced to resort to the same strategy. Conspicuously slower boats had defended in 1934 and 1962. Maybe it could happen again, even against these new challengers tested in the crucible of competition, even with the Louis Vuitton Cup representing a new tradition and a new threat to the defender. Even, as they well knew, against the odds. ◄

THE LOUIS VUITTON CUP

In 1983 the inaugural Louis Vuitton Cup gave challengers a structured series of competition in which they could hone their skills and improve their chances of victory against the America's Cup defender. As it turned out, that first event would turn the America's Cup community on its head, as the winner would go on to take the America's Cup trophy from the New York Yacht Club for the first time in the event's history. Just four years later, Dennis Conner would take the trophy back, but not before winning the Louis Vuitton Cup. And thus the saying was born: To win the America's Cup, first win the Louis Vuitton Cup. In this way, the Louis Vuitton Cup has acted as yet another guardian of the America's Cup, and has gone on to be one of the most colorful events in sailing.

LEFT: Prada Challenge dramatically forging its way to victory in the rough waters off Auckland, New Zealand, during the 2000 Louis Vuitton Cup. • TOP: Prada Challenge celebrates victory at the 2000 Louis Vuitton Cup in Auckland, New Zealand. • ABOVE: China Team during the round robin match against BMW ORACLE Racing during the 2007 Louis Vuitton Cup.

PAGES 72-73: Louis Vuitton Pacific Series 2009 Auckland, New Zealand. Following a day of racing, Louis Vuitton Pacific Series spinnakers hang to dry in the boat shed.

5

THE CUP CHANGES HANDS

MARK CHISNELL

I n 1983 the challenger and defender met for the twenty-fifth time in the America's Cup match, twenty-five times stretching across 132 years. It was the singular moment at the heart of every America's Cup summer. After the years of training, the months of design work and boatbuilding, the long hours of testing, mainte- nance, practicing maneuvers, dragging sails around, and washing decks, it was finally here. It was the moment when the defender and challenger sailed against one another for the first time. At last, the world would see who was faster.

So it was that at 12:10 pm. on September 14, 1983, Alan Bond's *Australia II*, with John Bertrand at the wheel, lined up against Dennis Conner's *Liberty* for the start of the first race of that year's match. There was nothing in it off the line, there was nothing in it halfway up the first leg, and there was still nothing in it at the first mark. *Australia II* led *Liberty* around by just eight seconds, and a collectively held breath was released. This time it might just be different. At the very least, it was a contest. The signs had been there all summer—*Australia II* had lost only five races out of fifty-four to the six other potential challengers. The boat was rumored to have a special, almost magical keel that had remained shrouded and been the subject of great controversy. Hope that this boat would be a match for the defender had never been higher.

Three hours and change later, the flame of hope wasn't extinguished but was flickering weakly, as *Liberty* crossed the line ahead of *Australia II*. It was a bitter disappointment. The defender slid past on the third leg, but the

PAGES 74–75: With the replica of *America* in the background, *Australia II*, to weather of *Liberty*, leads in what would prove to be one of the most pivotal races in America's Cup history. • RIGHT: *Australia II* crosses in front of *Liberty* downwind on the penultimate leg of the final race of the 1983 America's Cup.

ABOVE, LEFT: From above *Australia II* looked much like other 12-Meters, but underwater and out of sight is where the magic was. • ABOVE, RIGHT: Even in a slower boat, Dennis Conner and his crew managed take the Aussies to match point, leading 3–1 after the fourth race.

challenger had stayed in touch, made gains on leg five, and got into a position to attack. Then the steering gear broke. In the gusty northeasterly, it was all Bertrand and his crew could do to get *Australia II* across the finish line. The more things change, the more they stay the same, the watching crowds might have sighed.

If the refrain was repeated, it was louder the following day. The weather was similar, and in the breeze, the top of *Australia II*'s mainsail started to come apart before the start. Extraordinarily, and despite the problem, Bertrand and his crew managed to reach the first mark in front, but then lost yardage on the second and third legs when Colin Beashel was hoisted to the top of the mast to repair the sail. Conner could sniff blood now, and on leg four he closed and then passed in a fading breeze. The Aussies slapped a protest in for one of the American moves—but it was 2–0 at the finish line, and it was still 2–0 after the jury sat for six and a half hours to consider and then dismiss the protest.

It appeared to get even worse for the Aussies: They led the third race by almost six minutes before a weak wind failed completely, and the officials abandoned the race. Nevertheless, Bertrand knew that they had sailed away from the Americans, and on September 18 the tide turned. Conner made a mistake on the start line and handed a first-leg advantage to Bertrand. The Aussies rammed it home, winning by three minutes and fourteen seconds. It was the biggest-ever challenger victory, but much more importantly it was 2–1.

The fourth race saw Conner squeeze in front of Bertrand at the start and build a slim lead to the first mark. The *Australia II* crew hounded *Liberty* for the next three and a half hours, but it belonged to the Americans by forty-three seconds on the line. It was 3–1 and match point when the boats towed out into a much stronger breeze for race five. Now it was *Liberty*'s turn for the gremlins—the Americans broke a mast fitting an hour before the start. Scott Vogel and Tom Rich were hauled up to get rid of the damaged part, while the rest of

> "Design has taken the place of what sailing used to be."
>
> —DENNIS CONNER

the team tried to find a replacement. They just got it fixed in time, only to tear a sail in the rush to pull it up and get into the race.

The opposition was in disarray, and Bertrand had every opportunity to get a race back, but he proceeded to lose all the advantage by crossing the line early. It was a terrible error and could have cost *Australia II* the America's Cup, but it didn't. The American mast fitting failed again, and Bertrand sailed past a limping *Liberty* to win by one minute and forty-seven seconds. The Aussies had pulled it back to 3–2, but Conner still had match point, and the Australians needed to win twice more without a loss.

The sixth race was windy again, and again Conner led off the start line. The Americans didn't take the opportunity to play it tight and stay between the man and the hoop—or, in this case, the other boat and the buoy. The latter tactic, called covering, is most effective when the boats have at least the same speed. With a slower boat, covering can result in the opposition going straight past. But on this occasion that's exactly what happened anyway, as Bertrand and his

crew found the best of the wind on the first leg and led by more than two minutes at the mark. It got a lot worse for the Americans from there, and *Australia
II* romped away to a lead of almost three and a half minutes at the finish.

It was 3–3, and if the sixth race of an America's Cup match was unusual,
then the seventh was completely uncharted territory. No one had taken the
defender to a decisive, winner-takes-all since the 1920 match when *Shamrock
IV* lost to *Resolute* in a decisive fifth race.

ABOVE: *Liberty* (left) and *Australia II* (right) reaching to
the leeward mark and capitalizing on an increasingly clear
advantage.

ABOVE: *Australia II* winning the America's Cup and celebrating Aussie-style, beers in hand. The victory marked the end of 132 years of U.S. dominance.

"You get out there and you're as good as the next guy who might be a Vanderbilt. You get out there and all you've got is a common element—the wind and the sea—and everybody's equal."

—ALAN BOND

THE GRAND FINALE

After two straight wins, there was little doubt that the momentum was in the Australians' favor. Nevertheless, after three weak starts in a row, Bertrand decided to call a layday, a time-out, and *Australia II* spent the day practicing. Meanwhile, Dennis Conner took *Liberty* to a boatyard and stripped out internal ballast and added sail area to try to speed the boat up in the anticipated lighter conditions. The final race was scheduled for September 24, but the wind refused to cooperate. Everyone had to stew for one more day, and then another as Conner called for his layday—and went back to the boatyard for more tweaking.

On September 26, the two boats finally came to the line for the last time. Nerves were strung out a little bit further as the light breeze forced a postponement, and it was 1:05 pm before they got going. It was a split start, with Conner ahead off the line but Bertrand winning the favored end. *Liberty*, with its extra sail area and re-trimmed weight, was a different, quicker boat, but the Australians worked their start into a lead. Then, like the Americans the day before, they chose not to cover. *Liberty* was dead even the next time they came back together. Conner continued to gain and built a lead of about thirty seconds by the first mark. *Australia II* kept chipping away and over the next two legs pulled back a few seconds.

The wind eased, increased, and shifted on the fourth leg. Bertrand headed to the left-hand side of the course, and this time Conner didn't cover. Both skippers were backing their judgment and that of their tacticians and crews. This time Conner called it right, opening his lead to just under a minute by the end of the leg. The two boats rounded the penultimate mark in the soggy wind under the mass of spectator boats.

Liberty's sail choices were limited by the reballasting, and *Australia II* quickly started to make gains on a leg that had been its weakness earlier in the summer. Now the Australians' hard work on their sails was rewarded—they were faster, and with the Americans rattled, Bertrand and his team picked the better breeze. Conner wriggled like a fish on the hook, but *Australia II* sailed right past *Liberty* and into a twenty-one-second lead at the final mark.

All of Australia watched, spellbound, bleary-eyed in the early hours of the morning, as the boats turned for home. In a situation like this, the playbook said that Conner should keep maneuvering to force an error from Bertrand and keep *Liberty* away from the edges of the racecourse, where the positional game would be over and the leading boat heavily favored. So Conner threw forty-seven tacks at them up that final leg, and this time Bertrand covered every single one. The Americans had one last trick, dragging the race into the spectator fleet, but it was hopeless. *Australia II* had the lead, and Bertrand and his crew weren't about to hand over their place in history. The America's Cup was Australia's.

The triumphant Aussies returned to the dock, and after encouragement from the cheering crowds, Alan Bond gave the okay to finally drop the screens from *Australia II* and reveal Ben Lexcen's magical winged keel to the world. It was the final act in a drama too unbelievable to be passed off as fiction. But when the dust settled, only one thing mattered: The America's Cup was going to Australia, and sport's longest-winning run had come to a crashing halt.

ABOVE: Alan Bond giving the signal to reveal the keel. •
BELOW: Spectators thrill at *Australia II*'s keel after Alan Bond's grand gesture, and many float out on dinghies to touch what was sailing's equivalent of a talisman.

ABOVE: The crew of *Australia II* all smiles at the final press conference. • BELOW: John Bertrand (left) and Alan Bond (right) proudly accepting the America's Cup trophy.

BELOW: In 1987 Dennis Conner headed to the Southern Hemisphere determined to win back the America's Cup. Here his *Stars & Stripes* leads Australia's *Kookaburra III*.

AN UNEXPECTED INFLUENCE

New Zealand is the smallest nation ever to compete for the America's Cup. Yet, in twenty-seven years since entering the Cup arena, it has had a profound impact. New Zealander Sir Russell Coutts has won the trophy four times and heads the defender ORACLE TEAM USA in the 34th America's Cup. Emirates Team New Zealand, led by Grant Dalton, is a strong contender in the challenger group, and Kiwis are scattered throughout the event management structure and all the teams.

New Zealand's role in shaping the course of the competition began when Australia's famous 1983 victory in Newport, Rhode Island, brought the America's Cup within striking distance. With backing from merchant bankers Sir Michael Fay and David Richwhite, New Zealand made its debut in Fremantle, Australia, in 1987—and instantly transformed the state of the art.

Up to then, 12-Meter yachts had been of wood or aluminum. Keen to showcase New Zealand as a progressive, innovative economy, the team built the world's first fiberglass 12-Meter yachts. Known as the "Plastic Fantastic," *KZ7* won every match but one before being defeated in the challenger finals. Not content to wait out the customary America's Cup cycle, Fay issued an early and unusual challenge for a

ABOVE: Sir Peter Blake, center, and Russell Coutts, left, take the America's Cup to the island nation of New Zealand after defeating Team Dennis Conner in 1995.

ABOVE: Sir Peter Blake greeting the crowd during the America's Cup parade in 2000. Tragically, Blake was murdered by pirates in 2001 during an environmental expedition in Brazil.

one-on-one match in 1988. His challenge abandoned the 12-Meter class and returned to the 90-foot maximum waterline measurement stipulated in the Deed of Gift.

This turned into a mismatch between *KZ1*, the huge New Zealand monohull, and Dennis Conner's fleet-footed catamaran, *Stars & Stripes*. New Zealand lost on the water and in the bitter court battle that followed but once again had reshaped the event. The 12-Meters would never sail in the America's Cup again, replaced by the International America's Cup Class, which competed in various forms from 1992 to 2007.

In 1992, New Zealand produced yet another groundbreaking yacht featuring a bowsprit and double strut keel, which took the team through to the Louis Vuitton Cup finals. But their campaign faltered under a welter of technical protests against the bowsprit. By now, Fay and Richwhite had exhausted their ambitions. Revered ocean racer Sir Peter Blake took up the torch. Determined to avoid controversy, Team New Zealand's *Black Magic*, helmed by Russell Coutts, rocketed to a textbook 5–0 whitewash of Dennis Conner's 1995 defense in San Diego. In a century and a half, Australia and New Zealand were the only countries to break the U.S. hold over the America's Cup, and in 2000, New Zealand became the first country outside the United States to successfully defend the trophy.

TOP: New Zealand is reputed to have more boats per capita than any other nation in the world. A multitude took to the water during the 2000 America's Cup. • ABOVE: New Zealand's *Black Magic* crosses in front of Team Dennis Conner during the 1995 America's Cup race.

A NEW ERA

The impact of *Australia II*'s win was immediate and transformative, turning the competition into the fully fledged international event that it is today. Dennis Conner said years afterward, "Me losing after 132 years was the best thing that ever happened to the America's Cup. . . . Before the win by the Australians, the America's Cup was only big in the minds of the yachties, but the rest of the world didn't know or care about it at all. But when we lost it . . . it was a little bit like losing the Panama Canal—suddenly everyone appreciated it."

The victory (or loss) stoked international interest in the event like never before, and an amazing thirteen teams from six countries turned up in Western Australia to try to take the Cup away from the four teams contesting the defender's berth. A start-up sports television network saw an opportunity to make a name in the strong winds, bright sunshine, and big Indian Ocean waves. ESPN beamed the spectacular pictures back into American homes as Conner fought to right the wrongs of four years earlier.

OPPOSITE: *Stars & Stripes* ahead of New Zealand during the 1987 Louis Vuitton Cup in Freemantle, fighting to get to the America's Cup match and right the wrongs of the 1983 loss to Australia. • ABOVE: *Kookaburra III* heading out to the 1987 America's Cup finals to a cheering crowd in Freemantle, Australia.

Alan Bond's grand gesture in revealing *Australia II*'s keel came back to haunt him, as everyone else knew what they were trying to beat. In 1987, Bond wasn't even chosen to defend, and Dennis Conner completed his revenge when his *Stars & Stripes* returned the Cup to the United States, punishing Australia's *Kookaburra III* 4–0. The America's Cup had never seen anything quite like it. Millions of people tuned in around the world, joining the estimated hundred thousand spectators packed onto the beaches and breakwaters of Fremantle.

The blueprint for how to operate a successful team had also been rewritten. In this new era of America's Cup campaigns, building three new boats and sailing full-time were standard operating procedure. The newest idea was to have an internal design team, rather than subcontracting the creativity to an outside individual or firm. The concept poured fuel onto the technology fire, as the design coordinators hired more specialists to work in the ever-expanding areas of research and development. The bonfire was fed by faster computers and the greater potential for a breakthrough.

The design team concept was used by both Conner and the New Zealanders, his opponents in the final of the 1987 Louis Vuitton Cup. It was the Kiwis' first go at the America's Cup, and they went directly to the challenger finals, winning thirty-seven of thirty-eight races on the way. Unfortunately, they couldn't beat Conner once when it really counted, and lost 4–1. However, they introduced a new generation of sailors to the competition who would come to dominate the event for two decades and counting.

THE INTERNATIONAL AMERICA'S CUP CLASS

Dennis Conner had won but immediately made a serious mistake, prevaricating about the venue and the conditions for the next defense. Sir Michael Fay, who with his partner, David Richwhite, bankrolled the first New Zealand Cup challenge, saw an opportunity. Fay issued an individual challenge from the Mercury Bay Boating Club under the original rules of the Deed of Gift. The matter went to the New York State Supreme Court, which decided that Conner couldn't ignore Fay's challenge to race in a 135-foot monohull. Conner and his lawyers reread the Deed of Gift, and then he built a much smaller, but much quicker, catamaran to race against Fay's huge monohull in the 1988 match. Unsurprisingly, Conner won, and his lawyers won the rematch in the courts when the New York State Court of Appeals confirmed his victory in the uneven match.

The legal wrangling continued into April 1990 when the court issued its final verdict. In the meantime, much of the wider public interest had drifted away, but the America's Cup community had not been idle. When the competition finally returned to the water for a multichallenger match in 1992, it was in brand-new boats: the International America's Cup Class (IACC). This was another measurement rule, not dissimilar in concept to the 12-Meter rule, but the boats were bigger and much more powerful. It opened up a whole new can of technological worms, with new design parameters and new materials.

When the challenger and defender fleets took to the waters of San Diego in 1992, there were two defense candidates and eight challenging nations—the largest number to date in America's Cup history. Conner's star was on the wane, perhaps with the passing of the 12-Meter, and he was beaten for the right to defend by Bill Koch's *America³*, which went on to defeat Raul Gardini's Italian challenger, *Il Moro di Venezia*. A staggering number of boats were built—Gardini leading the charge with five new hulls—as the designers explored the new rule.

Every measurement rule has a sweet spot, a size and shape of boat that for some arcane mix of math and physics has a little edge on everything else. A boat built in that sweet spot isn't unbeatable, at least not when it's racing against others of the same type. When that happens, the finer details of sails, rig, and hull shape all count. But when a boat is the first to hit the sweet spot and is different from everything else, as was *America* way back in 1851, it's a breakthrough boat. When it's well sailed and equipped, it has every opportunity to dominate. So it was with Team New Zealand in 1995 and a boat designed by a team whose principals included Tom Schnackenberg, Doug Peterson, and Laurie Davidson.

Team New Zealand was a new entity, brought together under the leadership of Sir Peter Blake, with Olympic gold medalist and match-racing champion Russell Coutts at the helm. The boat they took to San Diego for the United States' second West Coast defense lost only a handful of races in the challenger series. It went on to defeat Conner 5–0 in the match. It's possible to view this as the start of the New Zealand era in the America's Cup, but it's less about the nation than the individuals. The notion of a national contest for maritime bragging rights slowly became watered down as nationality clauses in the rules

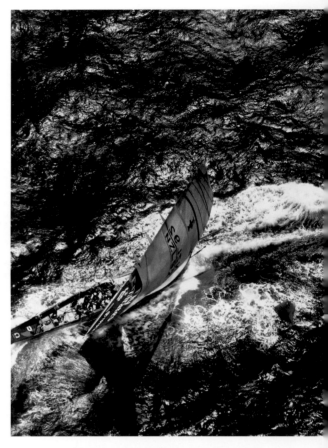

ABOVE: The New Zealand "Big Boat" was a technologically advanced monohull but didn't stand a chance against Conner's speedy, wing sail catamaran. In many respects, Conner's cat foreshadowed the future of the America's Cup.

were eased and then discarded, a process that reached its conclusion when landlocked Switzerland won the America's Cup from New Zealand in 2003.

New Zealand's glorious victory had initially led to an equally glorious defense on their home waters in Auckland in 2000. But unseen by outsiders, the team was already riven with internal tensions, and soon after the 2000 Cup, it splintered into many pieces, with multiple defections to opponents. Coutts led the strongest group to Switzerland and Ernesto Bertarelli's Alinghi team. They returned in 2003 to take the trophy away from their homeland with a 5-0 defeat of their countrymen.

The politics got rougher during Switzerland's first defense in 2007. After running a bidding process, Bertarelli had chosen to hold the event in Valencia, and the Spanish were treated to a remarkable sporting spectacle. Coutts was sidelined and left watching as his old Alinghi teammates raced his former Team New Zealand teammates for the trophy. The final seven, desperately tight races indicated the degree to which the major teams had reached a consensus, operationally and on the sweet spot in the rule.

LEFT: Alinghi outpacing Emirates Team New Zealand around a mark during the 2007 America's Cup match. By this time, the IACC yachts were being design with a remarkably narrow beam. • BOTTOM: BMW ORACLE during the 2010 America's Cup, a race that proved a sea change in the history of the event.

The teams were now chasing an ever-diminishing performance return through an expanding maze of technical research. Fighter pilot–style heads-up displays were built into sunglasses. Teams of people ran design and race simulations on supercomputers. Sails, masts, and hulls were all molded in carbon-fiber and required supercomputers to calculate the structures and loads. It was a process of endless refinement, and the contests got closer and closer until the final breathtaking race in 2007, when *Alinghi* crossed the line one second ahead of Team New Zealand to take the series 5–2 and defend the America's Cup. Then it all changed.

THE GAME CHANGER

In 2008, the game was turned on its head by Larry Ellison's BMW Oracle Racing, with Russell Coutts back in the thick of it as the team's head. They were unhappy about the fairness of Bertarelli's proposals for the next America's Cup. They were not alone in that, but they were alone in going to the New York State Supreme Court to force an individual match against Bertarelli under the Deed of Gift (DOG). Once again, the America's Cup would be decided by a DOG match in boats limited only by the most basic parameters cited by the Deed.

The design problems were now fundamental engineering questions. Would a catamaran be faster than a trimaran? Could a powerful, solid airplane-style

The design problems were now fundamental engineering questions. Would a catamaran be faster than a trimaran? Could a powerful, solid airplane-style wing be built reliably at the size required by BMW ORACLE's monster trimaran?

wing be built reliably at the size required by BMW Oracle's monster trimaran? The questions were finally answered in February 2010, when BMW Oracle Racing and the radical wing went up against Alinghi's giant catamaran and its more conventional soft mainsail. Bertarelli and Alinghi were defeated 2–0 by Coutts and BMW Oracle Racing and once again the trophy was headed back to the United States. It was the third nation that Coutts had won the America's Cup for, this time as CEO. Australian Jimmy Spithill shouldered the responsibility of skippering the fastest and, arguably, most extreme yacht the America's Cup had ever seen. Together, Coutts, Spithill, and BMW Oracle Racing had stopped Bertarelli's plans for the event, but the question remained—what sort of America's Cup would the 34th be? ◀

6

SAN FRANCISCO: PLACE, RACE, & THE 34TH AMERICA'S CUP

KIMBALL LIVINGSTON

For a walk on the wild side, the America's Cup had to come to the Wild West. For the ethos. For the physicality. For the hint of an oceanic wilderness that slips in on the seabreeze to haunt even the haughtiest penthouse parlor.

The full width of a continent separates San Francisco from the longtime home of America's Cup racing, Newport, Rhode Island, where *Summer* was a verb and, after racing, the crews relaxed on long green lawns or danced into the night in the arms of debutantes. Through its time in Australia, in the United States again, in New Zealand, and in Spain, the scene grew steadily more athletic and steadily more professional, but the revolution in racing that defines the 34th America's Cup ups the ante as never before.

Could Lawrence Joseph Ellison have imagined any of this when he was just one more student at the University of California, Berkeley, one more left brain learning coding, one more starry-eyed kid rigging a boat at everybody's favorite sweat-equity outfit, the Cal Sailing Club, and gazing out to San Francisco Bay? The lure was powerful, and we have to respect the sense of adventure that drew him along on the day that he truly discovered San Francisco Bay.

Cal Sailing offered Lido 14s in those days, hardy little 14-footers capable of surviving conditions well beyond their intended use. That was a good thing. Let's picture our doughty craft and its lone sailor clearing the Berkeley shore with all of San Francisco Bay opening to the west, 9.9 miles to the Golden Gate Bridge, 3,749 boatlengths in a Lido 14. As the day goes along, the breeze builds. This is the ordinary pattern in the sailing season here, and we are speaking of a journey that takes hours, plenty of time for the day to "develop." Beyond the halfway mark lies Alcatraz, once home but hardly homey to Al Capone, now a windswept mishmash of restored prison structures, decaying prison structures, and guano-coated rock. At this point, the breeze is stiff, but manageable, and the combination of seascape and landscape is dotted with iconic images. On one hand, there is the skyline of the city, and on the other, mountains rising away

"If we ever get the America's Cup to San Francisco Bay, we'll show the world how good sailing can be."

—TOM BLACKALLER

PAGES 94-95: *ORACLE TEAM USA 17* kicking up spray as if from unseen outboards and living up to its nickname "The Beast." • OPPOSITE: "Stadium sailing" is no hyperbole. The top of Hyde Street, San Francisco, yields a view of the Hyde Street Pier, the America's Cup racecourse, and Alcatraz.

to the north. But the lodestone pulling us forward is that bright red bridge that spans the entrance to San Francisco Bay, spanning also the passage to the vastness of the sea. For a sailor, it is fascination pure and simple to sail under that bridge. You have to do it. You just have to.

And the moment stays with you forever. The roar of traffic two hundred feet overhead. The rattle of wheels on the roadway. The startling shadow as you pass beneath. The howl of the breeze as it picks up. The sudden change in the world around you.

Let's be clear. The Golden Gate Strait, seaward of the bridge, is not always a howling maelstrom. But often enough, it is exactly that, and Lawrence Joseph Ellison, just plain Larry to his friends at Cal, had blundered into one of those

"I said, if God will just let me make it back under the bridge, safe in San Francisco Bay, I will never do this again."

often-enough. Call it a learning experience. The steep, white-capped waves breaking over the bow were too much for his little boat, and just finding a moment to turn—being broadside is the ugliest moment, the worst exposure—was an act of art, science, and dire hope. We know he made it, of course. In the process, he also made a bargain: "I said, if God will just let me make it back under the bridge, safe in San Francisco Bay, I will never do this again." And he didn't. But he also did not give up that part of himself that will boldly embark upon the unmarked path.

ABOVE: Larry Ellison details his vision for the 34th America's Cup when he brought the trophy home to San Francisco in Februray 2010. • OPPOSITE: The Golden Gate Bridge and Fort Point. The narrow strait between San Francisco and the Marin Headlands to the north creates strong currents and reliable winds.

THE VISION OF THE 34ᵀᴴ AMERICA'S CUP

When Larry Ellison's BMW ORACLE Racing team beat Alinghi to win the 33rd America's Cup in 2010, it was immediately clear that a new era in the America's Cup had started. Each time the trophy has moved to a new country with a new winner, the competition has evolved, but this would be on another scale. This would be dramatic change driven by a vision of creating an America's Cup for the twenty-first century.

The America's Cup has changed in the past, but never has it made a leap like this. New boats have been used before, but the AC72s, nicknamed "The Beast" and "Man-Eater," are a broad and unprecedented step forward. The race format and rules have changed, too, but never to such dramatic effect. The way the story of the racing is told has always evolved with the times, but AC LiveLine, the technology behind the new America's Cup television broadcasts, is more than an evolution; it has changed the sport.

"It's the America's Cup; it's not supposed to be easy."

Although both monohulls and multihulls were considered for the new America's Cup Class, it soon became clear that the multihull offered several critical advantages. The power-to-weight ratio of the new design would ensure eye-popping speeds. With little draft requirements, the boats could race inshore, close to spectators, providing a "stadium sailing" experience never before seen in the America's Cup. And the new design would challenge the crews physically beyond anything they'd ever experienced. When asked about the demands inherent in designing the AC72s and sailing them in a fast-paced, close-quarters format, Coutts explained, "It's the America's Cup; it's not supposed to be easy."

ABOVE: America's Cup World Series (ACWS) fleet race in San Francisco, 2012. The wind that blows from the Golden Gate Strait makes for a fast-paced reaching start toward Crissy Field, Marina Green, and the St. Francis and Golden Gate Yacht Clubs.

TOP: Russell Coutts explains the challenges of the new-look 2013 America's Cup. • ABOVE: Spectators who lined the shore got a close-up view of the 2012 ACWS action, something that would have been impossible in past America's Cup trials.

YACHT AMERICA IN THE U.S. NAVY

nted to, in business parlance, a hostile
saw the challenge from BMW ORA-
le. Ellison then became the final say
ncisco Bay, needs San Francisco, the
a. The bay is ideal, as Ellison always
evision scheduling and backgrounds
can hope to go large and stay large
find the leaders in sports graphics?
in an open-source revolution who
ce seven ways from Sunday? Right
will embrace any sports team that
proves itself worthy? You know the answer.

ABOVE: Luna Rossa, Artemis, and ORACLE TEAM USA run towards a cheering crowd and remarkable skyline in San Francisco Bay.

the temperature difference is enormous. The forces thus generated are likewise enormous. And there is just one sea-level gate. One breach. One wind slot. One opportunity to stage the 34th America's Cup in a place where summertime winds are as close to 100 percent reliable as winds can be and as powerful as you would want them to be.

The sailors of San Francisco Bay are a hardy lot. They have to be. They live with a regular diet of more wind than some sailors see in a year, and like it or not, they get used to the fact that the seabreeze is ocean chilled. But the bay, like the region surrounding, has its microclimates ruled by sheltering hills. Afloat or ashore, the northern reaches of the bay are a magnitude sunnier and

"A lot of very good sailors get in trouble when they get in conditions like the San Francisco Bay. I know that growing up on that, I can sail anywhere in the world."

—PAUL CAYARD

warmer than the wind slot, or the city of San Francisco itself, which has climates that vary from neighborhood to neighborhood, depending on whether they are sheltered or exposed. The wind slot is always exposed.

THE FIRST SAILING RACES on San Francisco Bay were the nineteenth-century races of working craft and their professional crews, but amateurs were soon in the game. Yacht races were frequent by the 1870s, and popular. The San Francisco Perpetual Challenge Trophy, a match race between two yacht clubs (sound familiar?), was first contested in 1895, making it the second-oldest match-racing competition after the America's Cup. There would have been a race from San Francisco to Honolulu in 1906, some 2,300 miles across the Pacific Ocean, except that when the schooner *La Palama* sailed into San Francisco Bay from the islands to consummate the plan, its crew found a city still smoldering from the great earthquake and fire. One year later, the city and its

PREVIOUS PAGES: ORACLE TEAM USA (left) and Artemis Racing (right). • BELOW: *Yankee* under sail. *Yankee* won the San Francisco Perpetual Challenge Trophy in 1956 • OPPOSITE: San Francisco from above. The Golden Gate Bridge in the distance marks the break between the Pacific and the San Francisco Bay.

sailors were sufficiently recovered to stage their first, less ambitious ocean race around the Southeast Farallon Island, 25 miles beyond the Gate. A schooner named *Yankee* won—on April 18, 1906, a nearly completed *Yankee* had been knocked off its ways by the earthquake—and fifty years later, *Yankee* won the anniversary race on that now classic course.

In the 2013 America's Cup cycle, sporting a white hull and green sail covers on her wooden spars, *Yankee* is berthed along the westernmost row of the San Francisco Yacht Harbor. Still actively sailed and raced, it is a living embodiment of local sailing history—a history that exploded upon the success of Larry Ellison's improbable challenge with his improbable yacht club. It is no secret that the Golden Gate Yacht Club was on the ropes, financially, in 2003 when Commodore Norbert Bajurin, in a stroke of inspiration, picked up the phone and dialed a number at ORACLE. The resulting conversation made the Golden Gate Yacht Club the challenging club for Larry Ellison's racing team, first in Auckland and then in Valencia. In 2013 they are the defenders, writing history for the twenty-first century and beyond. ◄

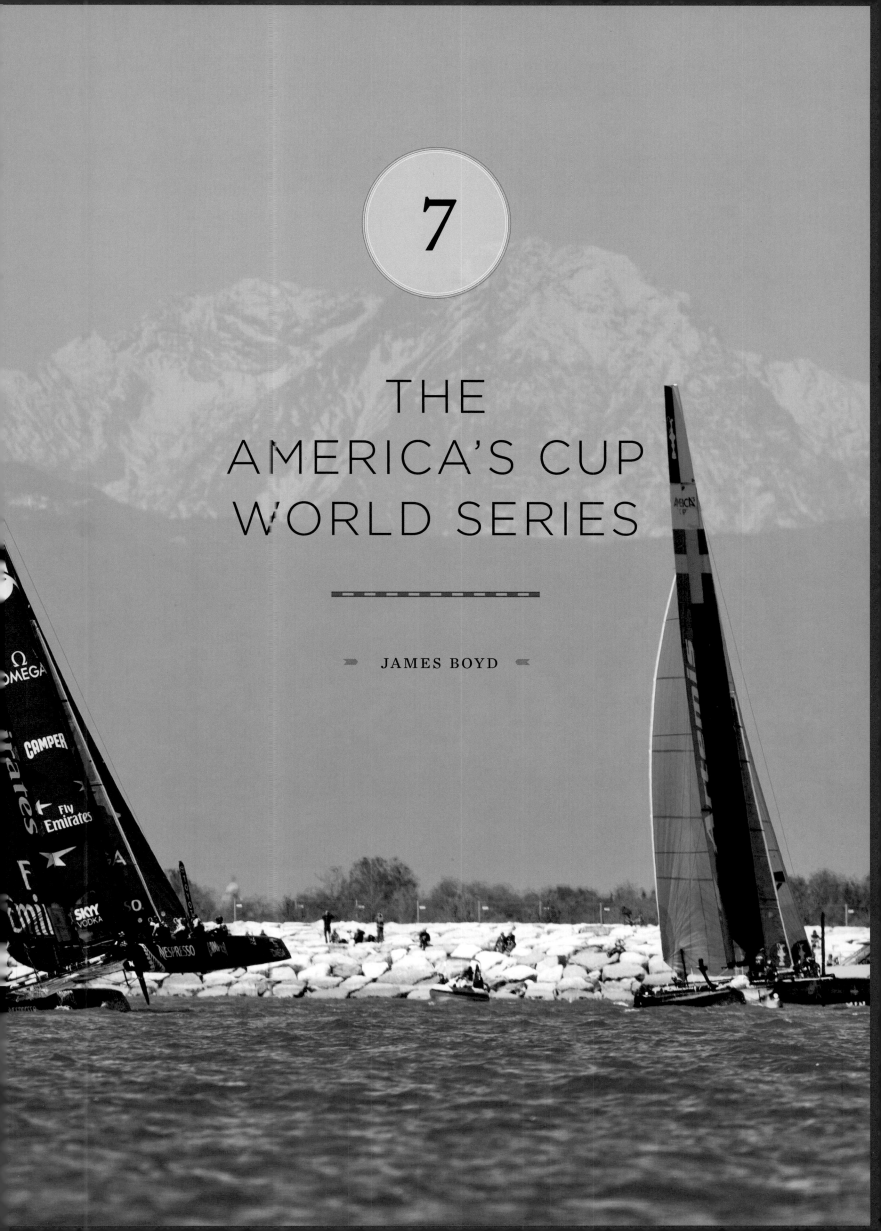

7

THE AMERICA'S CUP WORLD SERIES

JAMES BOYD

Larry Ellison and Russell Coutts's vision to revolutionize the regatta for the oldest trophy in international sport inspired a dramatic transformation from mono- to multihull racing for the 34th America's Cup.

An all-multihull competition that wasn't a result of a court ruling represented a first in the event's history. Beyond the gut reaction from traditionalists, the prospect of a multihull America's Cup caused concern from potential challengers who feared the U.S. defender would have an unfair advantage. Experience designing new-style boats and time with those boats on the water give boatbuilders and sailors an undeniable edge, and the American team had spent two years working on their multihull for the 33rd America's Cup. After reading the protocol—the mandatory rules for the 34th America's Cup—the challengers recognized that they had to buy into a new circuit and a new genre of yacht.

The aim of the America's Cup World Series—and the brand-new one-design wing sail–powered AC45 catamarans competing in it—was to help fast-track the teams' understanding of these radical new state-of-the-art craft and to create an "America's Cup Lite" circuit that would showcase the incredible

> "The new AC45 catamarans, the new race format, and the new rules are a great challenge."
>
> —RUSSELL COUTTS

PAGES 114–115: Energy Team France, China Team, ETNZ, and Artemis Racing. Race day one of the America's Cup World Series (ACWS) in Venice, Italy, May 2012. • BELOW: ORACLE TEAM USA Spithill, China Team, ORACLE TEAM USA Coutts, Artemis Racing, and ETNZ during day two of the AWCS Port City Challenge, San Diego. • OPPOSITE: Just off the reaching start the fleet of AC45s head for the boundaries during an ACWS race in San Francisco.

speed, the tight course layouts, and the spectacle central to the revolutionizing vision of the 34th America's Cup. Prior to the 32nd America's Cup, teams had competed in a similar "warm-up" circuit of events in Europe. But in the America's Cup World Series, they sailed different boats from the ones they would be racing in for the America's Cup itself.

For the organizers, the new circuit also provided the opportunity to develop every aspect of the competition prior to its incorporation into the America's Cup proper, including the creation of the best "made for television" yacht-racing event. Iain Murray, the dynamic regatta director and CEO of America's Cup Race Management, was ideally positioned to do this. Not only did he have a history of skippering yachts in past America's Cups, but he was instrumental in getting the high-performance 18-foot skiff racing on Sydney Harbour onto prime-time television in Australia in the 1980s.

Creating the AC45 itself proved a monumental task. The boat was drawn up by ORACLE TEAM USA's in-house designers. It was then constructed by their elite boat building team, Core Builders Composites, led by Tim Smyth and Mark Turner and operating out of a new facility set up for the purpose in Warkworth, New Zealand. Incredibly, with the help of many subcontractors from the New Zealand boating and composites industries, design to launch took just five months, even with the added complexity of "productionizing" the build to handle orders for more than ten boats for both the defender and the challengers.

OPPOSITE, LEFT: Race day two of the second San Francisco ACWS. The tight course layout required close-quarters maneuvering. • LEFT: Naples, Italy, presented the America's Cup World Series teams with rough, challenging conditions. • BELOW: Construction of the first AC45 catamaran at Core Builders Composites.

In August 2011, just six months after the launch of the first AC45, the whole sailing world and the America's Cup community looked on as nine AC45s lined up for the first America's Cup World Series regatta in Cascais, Portugal.

COMBINING MATCH RACING with full fleet racing and speed trials, the regatta in Cascais was unlike anything seen before in sailing. Small wing sail catamarans known as the C-Class race very occasionally, and this was the first time that a group of yachts as large as 45 feet fitted with giant vertical airplane-wing-type rigs had ever raced en masse. Anticipation among the spectators and viewers from around the world was as great as the trepidation among the fledgling crews.

Sailing the boats were many old hands from past America's Cups, highly experienced sailors such as former Artemis Racing skipper Terry Hutchinson, Emirates Team New Zealand tactician Ray Davies, and Artemis Racing CEO Paul Cayard who had to go back to school to get to grips with the high-octane new boats and their towering unfamiliar rigs. To help accelerate their learning, most of the teams brought in catamaran specialists from the Olympic Games or the Extreme Sailing Series. Even among the more seasoned multihull sailors, only Jimmy Spithill's ORACLE TEAM USA crew had ever raced with a wing sail before. As skipper Chris Draper put it—the wing sails were "a great leveler" between the teams.

Even the sound of the regatta was different—no flogging mainsails, no spinnaker drops, just the silent power and efficiency of the wing and the furl-

ABOVE: Arrival and unloading of the AC45 fleet at Quonset, Rhode Island. The entire fleet was transported by the freighter *Dolfijngracht*. • RIGHT: Cascais, Portugal, with its crowded beaches, sunny weather, and inshore racecourses, proved an excellent first venue for the ACWS. • BOTTOM, LEFT: Tim Smyth and Mark Turner of Core Builders Composites finalizing the build of the first AC45 in January of 2011. • BOTTOM, RIGHT: Cascais, Portugal, played host to the inaugural ACWS. • PAGES 122-123: AC45 fleet on the historic waterways of Venice, Italy.

ing headsails and the hiss of lightweight carbon-fiber hulls skimming across the top of the water.

As the America's Cup World Series went on tour—visiting first Plymouth, England, and San Diego, California, then in 2012 onto Naples and Venice in Italy and back to the United States with events in Newport, Rhode Island, and San Francisco—the racing format also progressed. For regular sailing fans, this came as another eye-opener.

Iain Murray and his race management team had come up with a new course format. Usually inshore yacht races are "windward-leeward": zigzagging into the wind and rounding a weather mark before heading back downwind. The new format involved a "reaching start," across the wind on the AC45's fastest point of sail on a short initial leg to a first mark. The twin-hulled speedsters would hurtle into this mark in unison, with all the drama of the first corner in a Formula 1 race. Traditionally, America's Cup racing was a defensive game, with the early leader trying to block and parry for the rest of the race. Now it was an attacking game, the reaching start producing overtaking opportunities straight off the start line.

For the AC45 crews, the game involved jockeying to find a position on the start line: Who could best "pull the trigger," accelerating out of the start the fastest, and then who was the most fearless rounding the first mark in the optimum position without causing a collision.

There was also a new element of physicality. Russell Coutts had promised that the AC45s would provide a thorough workout for the crews. With just five

sailors on board, the boats were short staffed. Another new feature of the racing that made them work all the harder.

In past America's Cups, racing was held out to sea, where the most regular wind could be found. ACWS courses, however, were as close to shore as possible, enabling spectators to view the action without binoculars. Plymouth Hoe and San Francisco provided perhaps the circuit's best natural amphitheaters for the AC45s, while the most confined course, directly off Venice's historic waterfront and piazza, proved both intense and spectacular.

ALTHOUGH SAILING IS traditionally a slow sport, AC45 competition is quite the opposite—as fast and intense as it comes, even in light winds. The ability of the AC45s to provide riveting racing even in mild conditions was immediately put to the test at the first ACWS event in Cascais. Although conventional yacht racing in such conditions would have been dull for spectators, the speedy catamarans were fully powered up in as little at 7 knots of wind.

And this was the principal reason for choosing the wing sail catamarans: They are very, very fast. Seeing a fleet of eleven boats (the fleet grew from nine to eleven over the course of the first season) screaming out of the start line and piling into the first reaching mark was the most exciting moment in all of televised sailing. Around the racecourse, the action came thick and fast, with crews unable to catch their breath before they reached a course boundary and were forced to tack or gybe. The crews were a blur of constant activity—trim-

ming the sails or the wing, raising and lowering the daggerboard and tacking or gybing sails during maneuvers, dropping and hoisting sails at mark roundings. And in big conditions, this all occured as they were being dowsed in spray flying back from the bow with the force of a fire hydrant.

In addition to all of this, the competitive nature of the ACWS was severe—unlike the AC72s to come, all the AC45s were identical, and teams had little opportunity to gain any technical advantage. As Mark Bulkeley, crewman on Team Korea, put it, "almost everyone can win races and hold good spots, so it means that it is just full-on. It is really hard to pull away and it is so easy to get sucked back in. You can be in third and you can get one tiny shift wrong and suddenly you are seventh, back in this group of six or seven boats that are fighting each other."

The ACWS may have been conceived as training ground for both the sailors and the America's Cup Event Authority, but it also proved to be a remarkable test of endurance for both the sailors and their AC45s, and a remarkable display of the new-style America's Cup racing—a million miles from the heavy-weight monohulls of the past lumbering out to one side or another of a giant triangle somewhere well away from land. ⚓

RIGHT: Crowds line the San Francisco waterfront between the St. Francis and Golden Gate Yacht Clubs. • BELOW: Loïck Peyron (right) helping Jimmy Spithill celebrate during the final race day in Venice, Italy. • OPPOSITE, TOP: Helmsman Chris Draper (left), skipper Massimiliano Sirena (front), and Luna Rossa Piranha crew celebrate in front of enthusiastic fans after their solid showing in Naples, Italy. • OPPOSITE, BOTTOM: Venice, Italy, was one of the most spectator-friendly venues of the America's Cup World Series.

J.P. MORGAN BAR

For just over three years, TeamOrigin looked set to be one of the strongest America's Cup challengers Britain had produced in decades. Unfortunately, team principal Sir Keith Mills didn't share Russell Coutts and Larry Ellison's vision for the 34th America's Cup and pulled the plug on his campaign in October 2010. This left many on Mills's team—notably Ben Ainslie, Iain Percy, and Andrew Simpson—free to pursue their campaigns for the London 2012 Olympics, resulting in a gold medal for Ainslie in the Finn class and silvers for both Percy and Simpson in the Star Class.

Percy was signed up by Artemis Racing, and Ainslie by ORACLE TEAM USA. Ainslie also chose to mount his own AC45 campaign, J.P. Morgan BAR, in anticipation of launching a full-fledged British challenge for the America's Cup in years to come.

Ainslie is a past Match Racing World Champion, but is best known for his record in the Olympic Games. After winning a silver medal in the Laser at Atlanta in 1996, he claimed golds at the next four Olympic Games, the last three in the heavyweight men's single-hander, the Finn. In 2012 in London, he eclipsed the record of Danish legend Paul Elvstrøm, making Ainslie the most successful Olympic sailor of all time.

Ainslie also chose to mount his own AC45 campaign, J.P. Morgan BAR, in anticipation of launching a full-fledged British challenge for the America's Cup in years to come.

BAR is backed by J.P. Morgan, a long-term sponsor of Ainslie's. It has strong links with ORACLE TEAM USA and thus BAR effectively represented a third opportunity—in addition to Jimmy Spithill's and Russell Coutts's teams—for the American defender to use the America's Cup World Series as race training for its sailing team.

Coming late to the scene, J.P. Morgan BAR joined the America's Cup World Series in San Francisco in 2012, immediately following the London Olympics. Although relatively green to the entirely new genre of boat, Ainslie is a faster learner. When AC45 racing resumed in San Francisco in October, he led for the duration of the regatta, ending up with a point total matching that of winner Jimmy Spithill—an impressive feat that bodes well for Britain's future prospects in the America's Cup.

ABOVE: Ben Ainslie polishing the wing his team's AC45.
• LEFT: The most successful Olympic sailor in history, Ben Ainslie (far left) was a quick study and helped his J.P. Morgan BAR team earn three fleet race victories in the October 2012 America's Cup World Series in San Francisco.

CHINA TEAM

Following their opening appearance in the 2007 Valencia event, China has become welcome, addition to the America's Cup community. Mastermind of the campaign is Chinese financier Chaoyong Wang, founding partner and CEO of ChinaEquity International Holding Co., Ltd.

"China Team truly represents the spirit of sports in China; while sailing is still a relatively new sport in China, we will be ready to compete against the best sailing teams in the world for the most prestigious sailing sports trophy," said Wang when he launched his campaign for the 34th America's Cup.

In the 32nd America's Cup, China Team partnered with the French challenger Le Défi, competing with a mostly French crew while providing some young Chinese sailors with the opportunity to learn the ropes at the cutting edge of competitive sailing.

Although unsuccessful in securing funding to a mount a challenge for the 34th Cup, China Team was a participant in the America's Cup World Series from the outset. Their campaign went through a number of transformations. Australian Olympic Tornado medalist Mitch Booth started out as skipper, then another Olympic Tornado medalist, American Charlie Ogletree, took over the position in Plymouth.

In February 2012, Ogletree departed the campaign, leaving the skipper's slot to become a two-way fight between experienced Frenchman Fred Le Peutrec, yet another Tornado Olympian but also with experience skippering 60-foot trimarans, and young Kiwi match racer Phil Robertson, who won the honor of becoming the team's regular skipper.

Since the 32nd America's Cup, the team has taken on all-Chinese management. The sailing team Robertson leads is predominantly from Australia and New Zealand but also includes two Chinese sailors: Cheng Ying Kit and the towering Ma Jian, who represented China in the Olympic Games in 1992 and became the first Chinese national to play competitive basketball in the United States.

Although fairly new to the game, China Team is making broad strides toward becoming a force in the America's Cup.

ABOVE: China Team skipper Phil Robertson. Robertson was a newcomer to the America's Cup but quickly proved his catamaran sailing skills. • LEFT: China Team's first training at the America's Cup World Series in San Francisco, August 2012.

ENERGY TEAM

With the 34th America's Cup being held in multihulls, it seemed only right that France, the leading national exponent of this discipline of sailing, should be represented. Joining forces to create Energy Team were brothers Loïck and Bruno Peyron, who have raced multihulls competitively since the early 1980s to become individually two of France's most successful offshore sailors.

Bruno entered the history books over the winter of 1992–1993, when he and the crew of the maxi-catamaran *Commodore Explorer* fended off two opponents to become the first to sail nonstop around the world in under eighty days, claiming the Jules Verne Trophy. Bruno was also the creator of The Race, a nonstop, around-the-world event held in giant multihulls in 2001. But he is best known for the Jules Verne Trophy and is the only man to have broken the record three times, culminating with *Orange II* in 2005, when he completed the circumnavigation in just fifty days.

Charismatic younger brother Loïck has won countless transatlantic races in his 60-foot trimarans *Fujicolor* and *Fujifilm*, including a double win in the OSTAR, a grueling, all-upwind slog from Plymouth, England, to Newport, Rhode Island. In Peyron's remarkable total of forty-two transatlantic crossings, seventeen have been solo. He has competed three times in the single-handed nonstop around-the-world race, the Vendée Globe, coming home second in 1989–1990. During the 33rd America's Cup, he shared helming duties with Ernesto Bertarelli aboard the *Alinghi 5* catamaran. But one of his finest hours came in 2012, when he succeeded in regaining the Jules Verne Trophy for the Peyron family, setting a new time of forty-five days and thirteen hours aboard the 140-foot trimaran *Banque Populaire*.

With backing from Swiss watch manufacturer Corum, Energy Team joined the America's Cup World Series from the outset in Cascais in August 2011. With Loïck Peyron alternating with former Olympic Tornado sailor Yann Guichard as skipper, Energy Team proved to be one of the class acts in the AC45s, winning the fleet racing in San Diego in 2011 with Guichard steering and again in Venice in 2012 with Peyron at the helm.

TOP: Brothers Loïck and Bruno Peyron of Energy Team utilized their multihull experience to prove the team one of the class acts of the ACWS, winning fleet races in San Diego, Naples, Venice, and San Francisco.
ABOVE: Ever enthusiastic, Loïck Peyron was quick to celebrate throughout the America's Cup World Series.

. . . the goal is not only to challenge for the America's Cup in years to come, but to win it.

Unfortunately, with the economic downturn in Europe, Energy Team was unable to secure the funding to go ahead with a challenge for the 34th America's Cup but has pledged to continue on for the 35th. Given that the Peyrons are two of the world's most experienced multihull sailors and given all the resources of multihull-mad France has to cherry-pick from, the goal is not only to challenge for the America's Cup in years to come, but to win it.

TEAM KOREA

On a continent where a new generation is waking to the notion of sailing for sport, Team Korea has unique opportunities. The country has coastline and harbors to the east, south, and west. The government is supportive and is driving investment in maritime recreation, and team founder and CEO Kim Dong-Young has chosen to catch the wave.

Originally a hopeful for competing in the Louis Vuitton Cup and America's Cup races, Team Korea in 2013 has refocused its energies on racing in the AC45 Class and building up its talent base. The crew, from the beginning, were not Korean, but the intent is to spark interest, train native Korean sailors to participate, and move Korea into the America's Cup game in the twenty-first century, which promises to be very much the century of Asia.

The team has represented the Sail Korea Yacht Club from its founding in 2011. At the launching and blessing of Team Korea's AC45, the ceremonies were handled as a traditional Jin Su Sik—much like a Western champagne christening, invoking the blessings of the sea god, Yongwang, through offerings of two Korean drinks, makeliki and soju. Led by Kim, the members of Team Korea each bowed three times, kneeling and touching their heads before the boat and tasting the potent drinks. It could not be otherwise, Kim Dong-Young explained, because "the sea god is one to be respected."

ABOVE: Onboard Team Korea as seen by wing trimmer Troy Tindall. • BELOW: Team Korea launch and shakedown, Cascias, Portugal, July 2011. Team Korea was new to the America's Cup but earned a second place in the first speed trails at Cascias.

ABOVE: The AC45 fleet moored in Naples, Italy. A common critique of the new-look America's Cup is that the cats don't have the majesty of the big racing monohulls of past Cups. But the spectacular and historic inshore venues of the ACWS seemed to more than compensate.

8

BEHIND THE
TECHNOLOGY
& DESIGN

JAMES BOYD

A BOATBUILDING JUGGERNAUT

As an island nation, New Zealand has strong connections with the sea and is reputed to boast one of the highest boat ownership rates per capita in the world. The result is that people view the marine industry not just as a job, but as a passion—and it shows in what they produce. In the forty years since New Zealand became a force in international yacht racing, its highly integrated marine industry has traced a parallel trajectory to become a world leader.

For New Zealand, often parodied as a nation of sheep farmers, even to contemplate taking on America's Cup teams representing the world's most powerful nations and backed by some of the mightiest technology companies was a bold step. Said Ross Blackman of Emirates Team New Zealand: "What fascinates people is that, as a small country with a rural background, we had the audacity to go and challenge for something like the America's Cup, which is essentially a technology race." Many of those teams and companies now buy high-tech equipment and expertise from New Zealand.

In the southern summer of 2010, New Zealand's high-tech Core Builders Composites yard produced the first hard wing sail AC45 catamaran. Then, involving a number of New Zealand companies in the production of components, the entire fleet of AC45s was built in New Zealand. In the southern spring of 2012, Emirates Team New Zealand led the way with the world's first AC72, built by Cookson Boats. And, in an unusual development, the Italian Luna Rossa America's Cup team utilized the New Zealand design for its AC72 and contracted New Zealand companies to build some of the components, including the arsenal of wings.

The expertise is not confined to race yachts but extends to luxury superyachts. Tony Hambrook, managing director of international award-winning Alloy Yachts, commented on the can-do culture: "Because New Zealand is relatively isolated, we tend to be innovative. We have had to be practical and figure out ways of doing things ourselves. That means we do not shy away from problems. We like finding solutions."

ABOVE: Team New Zealand's winning boat *Black Magic* defeated *Young America* in five straight matches to bring the Cup to New Zealand in 2007. • RIGHT: ETNZ's towering wing stands up to Auckland's tallest building, the Sky Tower.

Getting these various parts of the wings and their control lines to operate as the sailors and designers want them to is certainly an intricate job—but it leaves the crew in charge of wing trim with just three principal controls: the sheet determining the overall rotation of the wing, the camber (the angle between the main element and the flaps), and twist (the relative angle of the flaps to the main element up and down the wing).

Although the AC72 rule places strict restrictions on the design of the wings, the variations between each team's wings are principally in the distribution of the area between the main element and the flaps, the number of flaps, the fore and aft position of the rotation point at the bottom of the "main" element, and the control mechanisms.

THE FOILS

Although wing sails have played a part in previous America's Cups, the lifting foils of the AC72s take sailing into uncharted territory. Typically, the keel on a monohull keeps the boat upright, but also channels the power in the sails into encouraging the boat to go forward. Without the keel, a boat would slip sideways—an undesirable effect known as leeway.

To prevent leeway, a catamaran has daggerboards, usually tall vertical boards mounted halfway (fore and aft) up each hull in line with the mast. These are retractable, so that going into a tack, the board to weather (the side of the boat the wind is coming from) is lifted out of the water, and the one to leeward is lowered.

Since the 1990s, daggerboards have evolved so that they not only prevent leeway but also create upward lift. This has been achieved by increasing the horizontal part of the board, either through giving it a curved shape or how the entire board is angled to the rest of the boat. The vertical lift is important for

"Weight is tight and so forces the designer to trade things like windage for platform stiffness. The rule attempts to limit foiling by limiting the type of appendages and movable control surfaces on the appendages. The rule also allows the use of very stiff but quite brittle materials that require extra engineering effort to utilize effectively and safely."
—NICK HOLROYD

BELOW: Close up view of one of Luna Rossa's foils—a smaller feature of the AC72, but essential to creating lift, reducing the wetted surface, and making them fly. • RIGHT: Luna Rossa flying on their foils during a practice run in New Zealand's Hauraki Gulf.

performance, as it reduces the downward pressure on the leeward hull, greatly reducing speed-sapping drag, just as canting the wing up to weather does.

But the demands placed on these boards vary considerably, depending on point of sail, wind strength, and sea state. Working out how to make these boats operate to the optimum throughout the complete range of sailing conditions has been one of the AC72 designers' greatest headaches. For example, when sailing upwind, a vertical board is required to prevent leeway, but downwind, when leeway is less of an issue, a board is ideally more horizontally oriented to create vertical lift. In light conditions, a horizontal board is likely to create more drag than lift, and the horizontal component is best dispensed with. Trying to get all these features from a single board is an enormous challenge.

Such is the speed of AC72s that, in their development, the teams have entered some very experimental territory. Despite the AC72 rule being written to prevent the boats from becoming fully airborne, they have become fully airborne. Photos of catamarans sailing fast usually show them with their weather hull lifting out of the water, flying. Now, when the AC72s get above a certain speed, both hulls—windward and leeward—get elevated out of the water. This occurs when the daggerboards are used in conjunction with special inverted T-configuration rudders.

Fully foiling sailboats have been developed since the 1950s, mostly on the fringes of yachting. Hobie, the famous builder of mass-produced dinghy catamarans, at one time marketed the TriFoiler, a version of Russell Long's *Longshot*, which in 1992 became the world's fastest boat over a 500-meter course, averaging 43.55 knots. Since the mid-2000s, the Moth Class of 11-foot-long single-

ORACLE®
TEAM USA

AC72
131' 2" Mast Height

AC45
70' 6" Mast Height

Average Man
5' 10" Tall

handed dinghies has popularized efficient fully airborne sailing on foils. At the opposite end of the spectrum, Frenchman Alain Thébault has spent twenty-five years developing *L'Hydroptère*, a 60-foot-long trifoiler, which in 2009 became the fastest boat in the world, averaging 50.17 knots over 500 meters.

But the multihulls used for the 34th America's Cup and the new AC72s are the first occasions when the PhDs populating America's Cup design teams have focused their collective brainpower on airborne sailing.

To complicate matters, the AC72 rule bans devices that might improve the boat's overall flying ability. For example, many foilers, such as *Longshot* and the Moths, are fitted with a wand—a lightweight, hinged arm slung under the bow of the boat. This senses the pitch of the boat relative to the oncoming waves and mechanically alters the pitch of the lifting foil accordingly to compensate, ensuring a relatively smooth ride. With such devices prohibited, the AC72s have a strong tendency to hobbyhorse: The boat picks up speed and lifts out of the water as the foils start working efficiently, but then the boat continues to launch as the foils start working too efficiently.

When it comes to getting optimum performance out of the foils while meeting the AC72 rule restrictions, teams use one set of foils when the wind is too light to use the lifting foils, and another set when the breeze is up in order to get the boat airborne.

LEFT: Emirates Team New Zealand was the first of the America's Cup teams to achieve full foiling capabilities. Here the large daggerboard can be seen kicking up spray. • BELOW: Made up of more than 300 parts, the rigid AC45 wing sail replaces not only a traditional sailboat's mainsail, but also the mast and boom.

BUT THE QUEST FOR the perfect AC72 is not just about speed. With the short courses to be sailed in the confines of San Francisco Bay and with just eleven crew on board—compared to sixteen on the America's Cup Class boats in 2007—the AC72s must also be both extremely maneuverable and designed so that their crew can sail them efficiently.

As Dirk Kramers, ORACLE TEAM USA design team member, observed, designing an AC72 to obtain maximum efficiency from its crew is vital: "It is better that a boat can be sailed at 90 percent 100 percent of the time than at 100 percent 5 percent of the time. So the forgiveness in turning your boat is an important feature—if you come out of a tack slightly under or slightly over, it is not going to ruin your tack completely." Kramers believes this issue to be as important in the conception of the new boats as the wings, the foils, and the rest of the hardware.

For each team's designers, the AC72 represents a formidable new challenge. After five events held in America's Cup Class monohulls, the design teams were almost running out of new places to gain an edge. Improvements often came from several areas, each gaining a 0.01 (or less) of a knot. In stark contrast, with the AC72s, a single design tweak can represent a speed improvement of several knots.

For the 34th America's Cup, the AC72s are each set to have a sweet spot in their performance envelope in certain conditions or points of sail to a much greater extent than previous America's Cup boats. But an even larger contributor to success is the skill and control of a crew as they manhandle their waterborne, space-age dragster around an impossibly tight racecourse. ◄

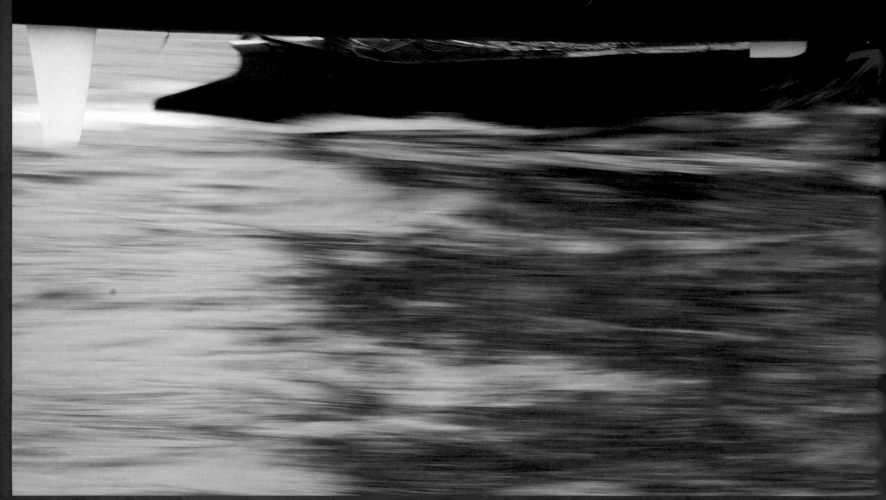

9

SAILING ON THE EDGE: THE DANGER

IVOR WILKINS

The America's Cup switch from monohulls to multihulls has opened a whole new dimension of speed and, with it, an entirely new element of danger. It has moved the event into the realm of extreme sport, with graphic images of fast action and sensational crashes inspiring frequent comparisons with NASCAR racing.

The very near loss of ORACLE TEAM USA's AC72 catamaran after it capsized in dramatic fashion in San Francisco Bay highlighted the danger in no uncertain terms. It was fortunate none of the crew was badly hurt as the catamaran pitchpoled in rough conditions in October 2012. They were plucked from the water as the team mounted a major effort to salvage the boat. Compounding their difficulties, the incident coincided with the biggest tide of the year and rescue boats were powerless to prevent the wreckage from being swept under the Golden Gate Bridge and out to sea. It was only when the tide turned and more powerful boats were brought to bear that the upturned hull platform was nursed back into the bay and recovered. The complex wing sail that powers these boats to incredible performance was totally destroyed.

It was a sobering realization of the consequences of capsizing these large catamarans. Learning about the incident, Grant Dalton of Emirates Team New Zealand, whose AC 72 was performing remarkably well and without incident, admitted, "that's the problem with these boats, you live on the edge."

But prior to the incident, teams had become used to capsizing the smaller AC45 catamarans used in the America's Cup World Series (ACWS) regattas and adept at quickly recovering them. A kind of "capsize culture" had developed where these accidents were almost celebrated as part of the general entertainment.

In fact, the ACWS played right into the NASCAR theme with checkered flags, thunderous music, and the burn, baby, burn appeal of wipeouts and crashes replayed time and again on TV promos and big-screen displays. It was

PAGES 152–153: Energy Team testing the limits of their AC45.
• OPPOSITE: Crewman Kyle Langford of ORACLE TEAM USA was able to hang on to the trampoline while waiting for a clear jump into the sea, avoiding the boat and knife edge daggerfoils 30 feet below.

sailing rendered as blood sport. "You don't have to go at 200 mph to know you are hauling ass," declared IndyCar rookie of the year driver J. R. Hildbrand after experiencing the sensation of speed on an AC45 in a guest outing on San Francisco Bay.

The change to something as radical as multihull racing in an event steeped in history and tradition was foreshadowed by the controversial 2010 contest between Larry Ellison's wing sail trimaran and Swiss defender Ernesto Bertarelli's elegant catamaran. In preparing for this match, Bertarelli's Alinghi crew made a pilgrimage to France, long considered the spiritual home of multihull racing, for a training session with offshore legend Alain Gautier. In a 20-knot breeze, the America's Cup pupils learned a quick and expensive lesson when they capsized Gautier's 60-foot trimaran, *Foncia*. Two crewmen had to be airlifted to the hospital, both suffering broken bones, and the boat sustained significant damage that took it out of action for months.

It was a sobering baptism that underlined just how quickly this form of sailing would punish the slightest mistake. Gautier noted that a similar error on the old-style America's Cup monohulls would have had minimal consequence. "On a multihull, the punishment is immediate," he said, adding, "a capsize like this is violent."

"On a multihull, the punishment is immediate, a capsize like this is violent."

Having won the 2010 match with a campaign directed by four-time America's Cup winner Russell Coutts, ORACLE software mogul Larry Ellison was

ABOVE: The tight courses and close-quarters action of the America's Cup World Series (ACWS) meant that a capsize often affected other boats in the race, not unlike cycling when a rider goes down in the pack. ORACLE TEAM USA Spithill getting a bit too close to ETNZ for comfort. • OPPOSITE, TOP: Skipper Jimmy Spithill (right) and trimmer Kyle Langford (left) talking over the dynamics of collision. • OPPOSITE, BOTTOM: China Team past the point of no return in Plymouth, England. This was only the second stop on the ACWS, and fledgling crews were forced to negotiate rough conditions.

ABOVE: Aleph, France, pitchpoling during race day two in Plymouth, England. The event was marked by eight capsizes.

determined to transform the Cup from a little-understood niche event to one with a much wider TV appeal. Fundamental to the transformation was an America's Cup in high-tech catamarans that would drive it into the realm of adrenaline sports.

AS A FIRST STEP, a fleet of identical AC45 catamarans was built north of Auckland, New Zealand. Would-be America's Cup teams embarked on an intensive exercise to learn the art and skills of handling these supercharged new machines, a process quickly marked by thrills and spills. Ironically, though, the first spill was not a product of speed.

The AC45 prototype undergoing trials by the Swedish Artemis Racing crew was completely stationary on February 21, 2011, as maintenance technicians attended to an equipment issue. Troy Tindall shared the job of test pilot in New Zealand with ORACLE TEAM USA's Jimmy Spithill, charged with introducing prospective America's Cup teams to this brave new world.

Tindall described how a "freak gust" caught them by surprise, and the boat did a slow backward flip, landing on its side and damaging the wing. "We are learning all the time," said a bemused Paul Cayard after the bizarre accident.

RIGHTING & RECOVERY

The high-speed, high-risk nature of multihull racing demands on-the-water pit crews who can make quick repairs and highly coordinated recovery efforts. "Every time a boat capsizes, it gets damaged," said Iain Murray, regatta director and CEO of America's Cup Race Management. "Getting the wing out of the water is usually where it gets damaged, not when it actually hits the water on the way down." The wing sail is fragile, and particularly in San Francisco when the wind kicks up big waves against the tide, the recovery process is difficult. An AC45 capsize generally means that the shore crew are in for a long night of repairs, but the boats have proved durable and able to take a lot of punishment.

When there is a capsize, the action plan is coordinated through the Race Committee boat. As Principal Race Officer John Craig continues to devote his attention to the race, Course Marshall Harold Bennett takes charge of communications. The radio channels are switched to emergency channel 16, which brings the medical crews, team chase boats, and Coast Guard boats into play. If crew members are in the water, the medical boats, which are jet driven to avoid having propellers near people, move in to recover them. On board are medics in wetsuits and dive gear in case they have to go into the water to assist recovery.

Meanwhile, the team chase boats take up station around the capsized yacht. One is at the bow to turn the catamaran into the wind. A second sets up on the windward side to take the prerigged righting lines and haul the boat upright. "Generally, if all goes well, that takes about ninety seconds to three minutes to achieve," said Murray. However, the eight-hour recovery of ORACLE TEAM USA's 72, during which the boat was never righted, proved the bigger boats would be a whole new challenge.

Still, many 45s encountered problems, too. On one occasion, Emirates Team New Zealand's wing filled with water, and it took more than an hour to get it back up, with considerable damage. The Spanish Green Comm team capsized close to the finish of a race in Plymouth. Righted without being head-to-wind, it inevitably capsized again in the opposite direction, putting it out of action.

ABOVE: China Team crew and ride-along guest find themselves in the drink and in need of assistance after capsizing during a practice run in San Francisco. • LEFT: Wing trimmer Dirk De Ridder is assisted onto an America's Cup chase boat by recovery crew after his AC45 capsized in an October 2012 ACWS regatta in San Francisco.

"We realized early in the first races that is doesn't take much to get out of synch on the AC45."

—TERRY HUTCHINSON

"This is the first capsize in these yachts," added the Artemis syndicate head, "but it won't be the last."

How right he was. The first high-speed spill came two months later on a blustery day in Auckland, when America's Cup officials laid on an experimental regatta to test course shapes and umpiring systems. During a hectic day of competition, ORACLE TEAM USA helmsman Jimmy Spithill and his crew all ended in the water after a high-speed capsize. "We were pushing really, really hard," he confessed with a boyish grin. "It was a good experience." It was, he predicted, an experience all the participating teams would share sooner or later.

Conditions on San Francisco Bay, home base for ORACLE TEAM USA, were typically boisterous in June 2011, when Russell Coutts put on a demonstration sail in front of the media. As principal author of this new-look form of the sport, he justified the hype with a dramatic forward capsize. Capsizing was becoming an occupational epidemic, and Spithill's prediction that all teams would get to join what became known as the "capsize club" would prove correct over the course of the ACWS. In fact, Plymouth, England, proved to be the toughest venue, with the effects of Hurricane Katia bringing strong winds into play. The event was marked by several collisions and eight capsizes—three in a single race.

To guard against injuries, the sailors wear protective suits, lifejackets, and crash helmets, a far different look and necessary change from the leisure wear and occasional foul-weather suits of previous America's Cups. In addition, fully equipped medical boats are constantly on station. Fortunately, injuries throughout the ACWS were rare and minor.

⬤———⬤———⬤

ALTHOUGH CAPSIZING LOOKS DRAMATIC, the wing sail acts as an air brake as the boat goes over, slowing its descent. "Because the wing stays rigid, it flutters down into the water quite gently," said Tim Smyth of Core Builders Composites, where the AC45s were built. In most cases, the boat lies on its side supported by the wing floating on the water. The exception occurs when the bows dig in violently, causing the boat to pitchpole, cartwheeling end over end.

TOP: "We were pushing really, really hard" admitted Spithill of his first capsize in an AC45 during a test run in Auckland, New Zealand. The incident occurred on the first test and refinement day in April 2011. • OPPOSITE: ETNZ struggled to right their boat after capsizing in Newport, Rhode Island.

China Team and Luna Rossa Challenge both had wipeouts like this, and the damage was extensive.

And, if the wing collapses, the slow-motion cushion is quickly lost. That is what caused the problem with the *Foncia* capsize. Although the 60-foot trimaran did not have a wing, its conventional soft sails initially provided the same air-brake effect. "We dug in, and the boat slowly went over," recalled Ed Baird, who was skippering *Foncia*. "Everybody was able to hang on. But the difficulty was that the mast broke in the water. Suddenly it wasn't slow motion anymore, and the hull slammed into the water upside down. In half a second we went from hanging suspended in the air to pushing upward to prevent the boat from crushing us.

"There were broken bones and dislocated shoulders. We had to get the helicopter in to airlift the injured crewmen to hospital, and we were slicing the trampoline to get at guys in the water. There was a lot going on, and this was a simple, mundane, daytime, non-racing capsize."

Tim Smyth said the build team has not kept count of the number of AC45 crashes and capsizes, but added, "We have been pleasantly surprised at how well the boats have stood up to some pretty rough treatment." Designer Dirk Kramers said the approach to the AC45s was to keep them relatively simple and conservative, recognizing they would be driven hard by teams new to

multi-hull racing. "The capsize rate is more or less what you would expect."

Because wings are relatively rare on yachts, historical data about their durability was minimal—and mostly discouraging—but Kramers says the AC45 wings have exceeded expectation. In most AC45 capsizes, the wing repairs are routine, unless they cartwheel or end up completely upside down, or if crew plunge through them on the way over.

As crashes and capsizes have become more commonplace, the systems for recovering the boats have become very slick. In some cases, boats have been righted in a couple of minutes and are able to continue racing.

SAILING HAS ALWAYS HAD ITS DANGERS. Look around any Grand Prix regatta and count the number of people with missing fingers or fingertips. This is an occupational hazard where lines and structures are under severe load. Head injuries, particularly from the boom sweeping violently across the boat, sometimes have fatal consequences. Drownings from falling overboard or being trapped in the rigging of an overturned boat are uncommon but not unheard of.

All these dangers remain a presence on the America's Cup catamarans, but there are additional threats. The speed of the boats alone heightens the possibility of injury. Capsizing is the most common accident so far, but there have been numerous collisions, some with boats riding up and over rival boats in the heat of crowded mark roundings.

In the August 2012 San Francisco regatta, Russell Coutts lived up to a long-standing reputation as "Crash Coutts" when he rammed the Race Committee boat after charging into a crowded start line and finding no place to go. "There was no gap there and it was too late to do anything about it," he explained before joking with the shore crew not to repair the damage too well, because it might happen again.

The crash threatened both Coutts's crew and the officials on the committee boat. Yet Coutts had the presence of mind to make a course alteration to hit the committee boat square on, minimizing the damage to his AC45. If he turned-up and made a glancing hit, he might have knocked the bow clean off his port hull.

No one was injured, but a portion of the starboard bow was left impaled in the side of the committee boat. "We were not able to extract it, so we covered it over," said Regatta Director Iain Murray with a shrug. He suggested it might have even added value to the injured boat: "When carbon is compressed like that, you make a diamond."

ALTHOUGH A CHEERFUL GUNG-HO attitude toward the crowd-pleasing crash culture has developed with the AC45s, the much bigger and more powerful AC72s are a different proposition.

Even launching them is fraught with danger. Raising the wing and attaching it to the hull platform involves complex choreography, during which the wing is extremely vulnerable, and the crew wrestle against its inclination to fly. "It is quite possible that severe damage is going to happen to a boat before it even gets in the water," said Grant Dalton, the Emirates Team New Zealand boss.

OPPOSITE: Simply being near the daggerboards at speed was often hazardous. • BELOW: Regatta Director Iain Murray points out the portion of Coutts's starboard bow left in the committee boat after the high-speed collision.

PAGES: 164-165: ETNZ skipper Dean Barker looks down as the team's AC45 clips the rail of an America's Cup committee boat. Notice the team's composure even on the brink of disaster.

On the water, these spectacular and highly refined machines are capable of 40 knots. As they defy gravity and rise out of the water on slender foils, they are on a knife edge; any loss of control could very quickly end in disaster. The consequences of two of them colliding at closing speeds of 60 or 70 knots—or pitchpoling at 40 knots, as was the case with *ORACLE TEAM USA 17* during that fateful practice run in October 2012—has proved catastrophic. The wing survived the pitchpoling. But as a hull flooded to prevent a swift righting of the boat, the short, steep waves of San Francisco wracked and wrecked the wing progressively. The wing was totally destroyed, and the hulls suffered relatively minor damage. The crew were fortunate to escape injury, but the capsize cost the team the one invaluable thing that money cannot buy: time on the water. Their 2012 training schedule, already reduced by earlier damage to one of the foils, was cut by at least a further two months.

Grant Dalton has firsthand experience of large ocean-racing multihulls (in 2001, he won a round-the-world race in a 110-foot catamaran) and also of Porsche GT3 motor racing. He understands the NASCAR comparison better than most and accepts the way the 34th America's Cup circuit has been marketed. But he cautions that the implications of an AC72 crash are much more dire. "In NASCAR, when somebody goes into the wall, everybody goes, 'Man, that's a big shunt!' and it is all very cool," he said. "But, there is a moment when that changes and that is when somebody gets seriously injured—then there is deathly silence. . . . That is the danger with the big boats. It is all very well, loving the capsize carnage, but the day somebody gets badly hurt, it is very different."

Recalling his *Foncia* experience, Ed Baird agreed. "To put it in perspective, if you crash a skateboard or a scooter, it hurts, but usually you just walk or limp away. If you are on a motorcycle and crash at highway speeds, you can do very serious damage very quickly. That is like the difference between these boats. . . There are a lot of dangerous things that we hope won't happen but *could* happen. They are taking greater and greater risks as the boats get bigger and the equipment gets more delicate and the speeds get higher."

Even in the absence of serious injury, the damage implications are huge. The 131-foot AC72 wing, larger than an Airbus A380 wing, is much more complex and fragile than the AC45 wing. When the Artemis Racing team broke their first experimental AC72 wing, more than three months were needed to repair it.

"It could be that a capsize in an AC72 could take you out of the competition altogether," said Iain Murray. "The damage to the boat and the cost of replacement would be enormous. The risk of injury would be very real." Sticking the bows into the water at 40 knots and going into a cartwheel would

"The damage to the boat and the cost of replacement would be enormous. The risk of serious injury would be very real."

catapult the crew in all directions. "It would be like those gadgets people take into the dog park to throw balls," said Murray. "It is a frightening thought." ◄

ABOVE: The tight course layouts of the ACWS, coupled with the eleven boats on the water curing later fleet races, led to several collisions and many more near collisions. Luna Rossa tries to escape the fast-paced chaos during an ACWS fleet race in San Francisco.

10

RACING
TACTICS

KIMBALL LIVINGSTON

A race in an AC72 catamaran is an emergency that begins at the start and finishes at the finish, if then. In thirty seconds, an AC72 can travel a third of a mile. "The fastest boats" is part of the mantra of the 34th America's Cup, and rightly so. But if you're riding that high-tech beast, if you're pulling on lines and reading windshifts and eyeing the competition and making bets in rapid order, you will be keenly aware of one additional fact. This is the shortest, tightest, most challenging racecourse ever devised for an America's Cup.

"Stadium sailing," the notion of presenting to a shoreside audience while imposing tight electronic boundaries around the racecourse—keeping the boats together for the sake of the live audience and television audience alike— is a game changer.

At Valencia in 2007, it was common to see two monohull opponents split tacks at the start and sail off to opposite sides of the course, one going left and one going right, until they were *4 miles* apart. And come back together, close or even overlapped, at the top mark. It was a boatspeed contest played out at a fraction of the speeds of the 34th America's Cup, with differences between the boats measured in fractions of that fraction. In those days, a tactician spent most of his time standing in the back of the boat looking around, assessing meteorology, current flow, and positioning relative to the other boat, and per- haps saying, "We'll be tacking in thirty seconds, twenty-nine, twenty-eight . . ."

Well, forget that. In 2013, the tactician is also part of the steeplechase— never a whole two minutes without a maneuver—that keeps every crewmem- ber's heart rate pumping full throttle. Before you can be a tactician in the 34th America's Cup, you must also be an athlete among athletes. And ready to adjust. The classic start, upwind to a mark dead upwind, has been around for

PAGES 168–169: Artemis Racing faced a number of design challenges and setbacks in the build of their first AC72. Here they put theory into practice during their first sail in boat one. • OPPOSITE: In America's Cups of the past, competing boats often found themselves up to four miles apart. Defender ORACLE TEAM USA Coutts and challenger Luna Rossa White cutting the distance to something closer to four inches during an America's Cup World Series (ACWS) regatta in Newport, Rhode Island.

generations. That's how everybody was trained, from Charlie Barr to Mike Vanderbilt to Bus Mosbacher, Ted Turner, Bill Ficker, Dennis Conner, John Bertrand, Russell Coutts, and Jimmy Spithill—and now it's gone. And that's only the start.

The new way of doing makes the race more of an attacking game, with more immediate passing opportunities and probably no safety for the leader. The race now opens with the wind blowing across the boat from the starboard (right) side. In the lingo, it's a "reaching start," with the boats on their fastest point of sail. At the two-minute mark of a two-minute countdown—don't be over the start line before the countdown reaches zero—the opponents enter the starting area from opposite sides, and already, there is a dynamic.

To a sailor, the world is wind.

To a sailor, the world is wind. Where the wind is coming from is upwind. Where it is blowing to is downwind. Everything that matters happens in this dimension. The sailor inhabits the wind by instinct, feels it in the hairs of the neck, sees its effect on the surface of the water, and feels it in the reaction of the boat. At every moment, depending upon the boats' positioning relative to the wind and relative to each other, one boat has the right-of-way. As they maneuver, the right-of-way advantage can shift rapidly and dramatically. That is the drama of the prestart dance.

BELOW: Spithill manning the tiller and traveler of his AC45. • OPPOSITE, TOP: ORACLE TEAM USA Coutts crew hiking out for ballast on the weather rail during the third day of racing at Newport, Rhode Island. • OPPOSITE, BOTTOM: Artemis Racing was the only team to launch their first AC72 without foiling capabilities. The AC72 rule was written to limit foiling, but early trials of the 72s suggested that the capacity to fully foil would prove paramount in the quest for the Cup.

RACING MONOHULLS VS. MULTIHULLS

Although both involve the wind and water, the differences between competing in the heavyweight Version 5 America's Cup Class (ACC) yachts and the latest lightweight, ultrafast AC72s are immense. This is mostly due to the physical attributes of each genre of yacht.

Being heavier, ACC boats are better behaved when maneuvering, tacking, gybing, and rounding marks, using their momentum and inertia to carry them through turns. Catamarans are slower to tack, typically coming to a near stop, but they accelerate out much faster. Surprisingly, studies conducted by the teams show that the distance lost in a tack is similar for the two types of boat, only on a catamaran, maneuvers must be carried out flawlessly, as the boat is much less tolerant of errors.

Former Artemis Racing skipper Terry Hutchinson gave an indication of the issue: "If your boat goes 4 knots slower in a straight line but accelerates twenty seconds faster [out of a tack/gybe], there is quite a trade-off there, and if it is three minutes to either boundary, you are a minute and a half on a tack and you are never going to quite reach the full speed potential of the boat."

Typically, on their way around the racecourse, the tacticians aboard the two types of boat look out for different things on the water. On the heavyweight monohulls, they are perpetually hunting for favorable windshifts that will allow them to sail a better angle and thus a shorter course to the next mark. On multihulls, because of their immense pace and the "apparent wind speed" (the combination of the true wind speed combined with the speed of the boat) this creates on board, even when they are technically sailing downwind, the wing and their softsails are trimmed in hard as if they were going upwind. Because of this the tactical teams gain more advantage if they can find more "pressure" than their rival—be it a gust or a building wind.

With all the crew so occupied sailing the boat, precious little opportunity is left for anyone other than the helmsman to gauge the wind and contemplate tactics.

For the sailing teams, the game has also changed considerably due to the tight layout of the course for the 34th America's Cup and the all-consuming effort required by the crew to manhandle their viciously fast AC72s around it. The high-performance nature of the AC72s, and the high price crews pay for any mistakes, means not only greater reward for good crew work but also more opportunity for lead changes during a race.

But regardless of the changes in boats and tactics, getting the best start and picking the first shift will ultimately pay, just as it always has.

OPPOSITE, TOP: ORACLE TEAM USA Spithill cutting it close while rounding a mark boat in Newport, Rhode Island. • OPPOSITE, BOTTOM: Though behind Luna Rossa breaks from ORACLE TEAM USA in search of cleaner wind while rounding a leeward mark.

On the countdown clock, from their opposite sides, both boats cross the start line and enter the start box with two minutes to go. One is required to enter on starboard tack, with right-of-way, and the other is required to enter on port tack as the give-way vessel. The Race Committee will position the marks to allow a well-handled give-way vessel a reasonable chance of making a clean, clear crossing in front of its opponent. If the give-way boat can successfully cross in front, its disadvantage is neutralized, and the game is on. If it fails to cross, the game is on anyway. Welcome to the jungle.

John Kostecki, tactician to ORACLE TEAM USA, said, "Coming in on port tack, whether or not you can get across the other guy depends on just how the line is set, and what the wind does, and of course getting the timing right. If you make it across, you have the freedom to decide when you want to come back and approach the line. The other guy will have to decide whether he thinks you're late or early. If you're late, he'll want to go in front of you. If you're early, he'll want to go behind."

It's a two-boat race, so the critical thing is to be ahead of the other boat, preferably at the start but especially rounding the first mark and entering the open legs of the course. Between the start and mark one, the reach is a mad dash, mere seconds, that more often than not favors the boat to leeward, on the left, which will be the "inside" boat at the rounding. Often, the prestart

BELOW: Because of the stiffness of the wing sails, they cannot be trimmed by eye, and during the ACWS it became standard practice to preset the wing for each leg of the race. Here Francesco Bruni of Luna Rossa trim the camber in the wing. • OPPOSITE: Luna Rossa crew hiking out during an ACWS regatta in Naples. The hiking strap and foot straps allow sailors to lean well over the hull for ballast.

TRIMMING THE WING

Trading a mainsail for a wing sail is no minor matter. The wing develops 30 to 40 percent more power per square foot than its fabric counterpart. At the same time, it reduces sheet loads drastically, because the wing just stands there; it doesn't require leech tension to create shape. It also looks good all the time, unlike a soft sail, which just plain looks wrong when it is badly trimmed. With a wing, the trimmer has to relearn his craft. Trimming by eye does not apply.

As the newest AC72s have come along, each new wing has had something new to teach. Each team, however, has climbed the learning curve with skill sets transferred from AC45 racing, where they established it as standard practice to preset the shape of the wing for each leg. This is entirely different from the continual retrimming of the mainsail on a conventional boat, but on wing sail cats there simply is no time for that. There is an adage: A sailor always looks up. Because aloft is where things happen; that is where your sail power is interacting with the wind. But on a wing sail catamaran, the trimmer must always, always be looking ahead for the next puff of breeze, the next wave that might require instant depowering.

Camber describes the shape of an aerofoil as the angle of its parts in relation to each other. In the wing sail, camber varies from a less-rounded shape ("flatter," to a sailor) to a more-rounded shape ("deeper," to a sailor). The flatter shape is for going upwind; on AC45s this means an angle between the forward and aft wing elements of about 17 degrees. When the boat turns downwind (outrunning the wind downwind, the crew still feels wind in their faces), the trimmer opts for a deeper shape, an angle between forward and aft wing elements of as much as 40 degrees on an AC45. When it comes to AC72s, teams guard their numbers and their techniques as state secrets.

The second factor in wing shape is twist, which is about creating a differential shape, bottom to top, with the upper panels of the wing more open, or twisted off, to account for different wind direction aloft and to spill excess power. In AC45s competing in a medium to heavy breeze, trimmers set the wing for 33 degrees of twist. Light air calls for less twist, and in very light air, the trimmer might employ zero twist, not because that configuration is aerodynamically correct, but to maximize power high up in an effort to lift the weather hull and reduce water resistance. The extra complications in the AC72s are heavy on the "extra," in part because these 72-footers employ more complex wing elements.

It's about seeing waves and seeing wind over waves and foreseeing the next emergency and responding before it becomes *an emergency*.

But wait. We've said that the trimmer presets the wing for each leg. It can't stop there. If there is no time to look up, only time to look ahead, what's going on? The third dimension of trim is rotation, allowing the whole structure to swivel out, away from the wind, for less power in the puffs—much less power if the driver stuffs a wave—or pulling it back in for more power. That's the trimmer's job, and it moves fast and there's never a break: It's about seeing waves and seeing wind over waves and foreseeing the next emergency and responding before it becomes *an emergency*. It's about doing all the above while working at a very high heart rate, while taking water in the face, in a competitive environment in which foils have taken speed, tactics, and physicality—the entire race—to another level, literally.

OPPOSITE: Inspecting the wing—the same that was subsequently destroyed during ORACLE TEAM USA's infamous capsize—during an early training session in October 2012.

maneuvering is about claiming that position and asserting control. "You look for the spot on the start line that is shortest distance to the mark, on your fastest point of sail," Kostecki said. "If you get that, and you're tight to leeward of the other boat, that's ideal. On such a short leg there is no way they're going to sail all the way around you and pass."

There are other possibilities. Sail enough races, and there will be times when one boat separates upwind and has a faster angle to the mark (*leverage* is the sailor's term) and gets there first. Not often, but it happens. With only two minutes on the countdown, inside the start box, the decisions come fast and furious.

The shape of the new America's Cup course developed through experiments in AC45 Class racing over the last two years. That reaching start would have been heresy just a few years ago. It is unique to the 34th America's Cup. The main portions of the course are more familiar to racing sailors: At the top and bottom of the course is a "gate," and each gate consists of two marks a distance apart. The tactician can choose to round either mark and go left or go right. One mark or the other will always represent a way to minimize maneuvers and maximize speed, but perhaps there is a reason to go the other way. Perhaps one side of the course has better wind or current, enough to pay off an extra tack or gybe. Or perhaps, no matter what else is going on, it is absolutely necessary to get away from a boat ahead and roll the dice by sailing in a different patch of water.

"It is yet to be established that eleven crew can really sail an AC72 hard and efficiently!"
—NICK HOLROYD

By multihull standards, AC72s maneuver well. Even so, every tack and every gybe slows the boat and costs distance. An important feature of the tactician's job is to minimize maneuvers. If he can force the other boat to make an extra maneuver, that's huge. The no-brainer way to minimize maneuvers is to sail all the way to the electronic boundary of the course before making a turn, but there is no such thing as a no-brainer strategy that will get you all the way around the course. Luna Rossa's Francesco Bruni saw a stark comparison to the monohull racing at Valencia in 2007, where there were "perhaps twenty decision points between the start and the finish. If you made a mistake, there was a chance that you could make a couple of tacks or a gybe and correct it. Now, there are half that many decision points, and each decision is weighted heavily. If there is a windshift that persuades you to not go to the boundary, then you probably will be bouncing from that point on. If it's a mistake, you will have to live with it to the next decision point. You can't just change your mind and throw in a couple of extra tacks. The price outweighs any possible benefit."

"Eleven crew on one of these boats creates a huge number of challenges. In every maneuver you have multiple jobs that need to be performed, and balancing that limited resource is not easy."
—DEAN BARKER

ABOVE: ETNZ's AC72 has four pedestal grinders on each hull for a total of eight crew grinding at any one time, which leaves only three sailors to manage winches and hydraulics. If the five-man crew of the AC45s pushed the limits, the eleven-man crew of the much larger and more powerful AC72s verges on unmanageable.

The imperative is to minimize maneuvers, and with that in mind, we can reel this account back to the first mark and consider why, most of the time, a boat will turn downwind without gybing and head for the right-hand side of the course (looking downwind). Simply put, that's the fast way to go. Even the trailing boat is likely to take that route, unless its tactician sees a big-stakes advantage in wind direction or wind strength on the left-hand side of the course. Such an advantage would have to be worth at least three or preferably four boatlengths to justify the cost of the maneuver. Water flow could also force a decision. With one-sixth of all the water in San Francisco Bay going out and in twice a day, currents here are powerful, more so than in most places where boats race. If there is a 3-knot differential in water flow between the left and right sides of the course, the tactician probably cannot ignore it, even if his boat is going 30 knots (3 knots being one-tenth of 30). If the trailing boat gybes at the first mark and goes left, the lead boat can cover the move or not, but if the trailing boat gybes to match, it probably will settle in for a few seconds first, rather than slam the maneuver. "If there's any doubt," said Kostecki, "go to the boundaries."

. . . everything about the 34th America's Cup is pushing the boundaries of sailing. These are boats that are capable of flipping end over end. These are boats that will show closing speeds of 60, 70, 80 miles per hour.

No one wants to break the electronic boundaries of the course—that's a costly foul—but everything about the 34th America's Cup is pushing the boundaries of sailing. These are boats that are capable of flipping end over end. These are boats that will show closing speeds of 60, 70, 80 miles per hour. This is a new world, and with a final reaching leg to the finish line from the bottom of the course, the races finish for the crowd and the cameras "around the corner" at Pier 27, where the press awaits them, and the fans, and happiness or failure. Once upon a time, Dennis Conner became the most famous sailor in the world by losing the America's Cup. That's off the table. The only option now is to win. ◄

11

THE CHALLENGERS & THE DEFENDER

KIMBALL LIVINGSTON

THE CHALLENGER OF RECORD: ARTEMIS RACING

Torbjörn Törnqvist made a rapid ascent from his start in sailing. Beginning in 2005, his combination of leadership skills and strategic acumen led Artemis Racing to championships in the hard-fought TP52 and RC44 fleets and inspired the team's confidence to challenge for the America's Cup. Soon after the Cup arrived in San Francisco, Törnqvist made the announcement that he would challenge on behalf of KSSS, Kungliga Svenska Segel Sällskapet, an institution founded in 1830. In English, it's the Royal Swedish Yacht Club, and today it has five thousand members across Sweden.

When Italy's Mascalzone Latino stood down, citing Europe's economic downturn, Artemis Racing became the Challenger of Record for the 34th America's Cup. This could be heady stuff for a first-time challenger, but the team's CEO, Paul Cayard, brings a wealth of experience. The round-the-world race winner and 1998 U.S. Yachtsman of the Year crewed American hopefuls in 1983 as a trimmer and in 1987 as tactician. He skippered an Italian challenger in 1992 and then helmed the defender for skipper Dennis Conner in the 1995 loss to New Zealand. He skippered an American challenger in 2000, served as sports director for the Spanish team in 2007, and in 2009 joined Törnqvist's already successful Artemis Racing.

It was a short stretch for Cayard to return to the America's Cup arena, and as the team turned the corner from AC45s and the training moved to developing the team's first AC72 and planning the next, Artemis brought in young Olympic 49er gold medalist Nathan Outteridge—whose short time as skipper of Team Korea had proved his abilities in wing-sailed catamarans—and Loïck

PAGES 184-185: The America's Cup trophy at sunrise in San Francisco Bay.

OPPOSITE: After several delays, Artemis Racing, the Challenger of Record, finally launched their AC72 on November 3, 2012.

OPPOSITE, TOP: Artemis Racing CEO Paul Cayard at the helm during the team's first sail. • OPPOSITE, BOTTOM: Artemis Racing team in Alameda, California during the much-anticipated launch of their first AC72 in November 2012. • TOP: Like defender ORACLE TEAM USA, Artemis Racing chose to stay in the Bay Area to develop and build their AC72s, allowing both to train on San Francisco Bay.

Peyron, a charismatic sailor with thirty-five years of big multihull experience. This pair came at the expense of Artemis Racing's first and principal skipper, Terry Hutchinson, who stepped aside in November 2012. "Terry gave nothing less than 110 percent," explained Cayard, but with unexpected hiccups in launching and sailing their first 72, the team had to focus efforts on accelerating its program. In a sport Hutchinson himself explained as "a game of inches," something brought home when his team lost race seven by one second in the 2007 America's Cup, every decision, or indecision, counts.

EMIRATES TEAM NEW ZEALAND

The team's DNA extends all the way back to Fremantle in 1987 and the Kiwis' first attempt to win the America's Cup as New Zealand Challenge. They morphed into Team New Zealand in 1995, in San Diego, when *Black Magic* won the trophy in five straight races. Five years later New Zealand became the first country outside the United Sates to successfully defend. In 2007, with Dean Barker at the helm, a bit of rebranding, and Emirates as a partner, Emirates Team New Zealand defeated Luna Rossa 5–0 to win the Louis Vuitton Cup finals and then won two of seven races in the America's Cup match against the defender, Alinghi. No other team at the 34th America's Cup has such a long, solid thread to its history.

The proud Royal New Zealand Yacht Squadron has probably produced more of the world's top sailors, per capita, than any other sailing institution.

The proud Royal New Zealand Yacht Squadron has probably produced more of the world's top sailors, per capita, than any other sailing institution—a cast of characters ranging from Olympians to ocean racers to the best of America's Cup skippers.

TOP: ETNZ skipper Dean Barker. • ABOVE: ETNZ in full gear during an early AC72 training session.

TOP: Emirates Team New Zealand under sail and foiling on *NZL5.* • ABOVE: ETNZ design boss Nick Holroyd working out the technical details of the team's big cat.

New Zealand suffered a demoralizing inflection point in 2003, when the team lost the trophy. But that was then, and this is now. Under the guidance of battle-hardened Grant Dalton, a veteran of seven round-the-world races, ETNZ today operates as a disciplined cadre of professionals. They even have a business model. Significant funding comes from the government of New Zealand, which speaks volumes for the place that sailing holds in the hearts of the citizens of that country, and Emirates airline remains the lead sponsor.

ETNZ was the first team to launch an AC72 and the first to "lift off" on foils. With the move from monohulls to multihulls, Barker said, "We've moved from a world of detailing and fine-tuning to an open book with fresh, clean paper. There are no stupid questions or ideas. We're just scratching the surface of a huge, uncharted territory. You'll have to have your wits about you to get around the course, but Emirates Team New Zealand exists for the America's Cup. We've weathered the storm since 2007 to give ourselves the opportunity to compete in 2013."

LUNA ROSSA

Between the genesis of America's Cup racing in the Solent on August 22, 1851, and the genesis of Luna Rossa's quest for the America's Cup lay a period of 145 years, five months, and twelve days. It happened in a moment of inspiration at a design meeting in Milan, not far from the marble Duomo that every visiting tourist knows. But for once, this design meeting in the fashion capital of Italy was not about couture. The chief executive of the house of Prada, lifelong sailor Patrizio Bertelli, meant to be shaping plans for a new cruising yacht when Argentinian designer Germán Frers exclaimed, "Why don't we do the America's Cup?"

In that moment, Prada Challenge was born, as was Luna Rossa, the team of the Red Moon. Bertelli could not know that, by 2013, he would become the first Italian inducted into the America's Cup Hall of Fame.

First, however, Prada would experience an unforgettable introduction to the game at the 2000 match in New Zealand. Eleven challengers from seven nations gathered to test their fortunes on the waters of the Hauraki Gulf. Skipper Francesco de Angelis won thirty-eight of forty-nine challenger races to claim the Louis Vuitton Cup on a high note. Then, in the America's Cup, came an 0–5 loss to the defenders, Team New Zealand, in their prime. It was a rousing opening act, nonetheless, and the first occasion in which an American boat was absent from the America's Cup match. It was also the first outing in this arena for an Italian helmsman and a performance worthy of the place on the world stage of fashion house Prada.

BELOW: Luna Rossa skipper Max Sirena inspects the stylish hull of the team's AC72. • OPPOSITE: Luna Rossa bearing away during an early AC72 training session.

Bertelli has fielded teams in each Louis Vuitton Cup since. In 2007, racing in Valencia, Spain, Luna Rossa made the final four. However, weighing the legal wrangling, delays, and bad blood that followed the 2007 races, he chose to wait on the sidelines until he could see AC45s on the water and a solid plan in place for racing on San Francisco Bay in AC72s. To reenter the game in 2011, leveraging a partnership with Emirates Team New Zealand, was a fortunate stroke for both. Luna Rossa poured in a welcome dose of funding, and the work already done on design and engineering by the Kiwis became available to the Italians. Luna Rossa's AC72 for the 2013 Louis Vuitton Cup shares the basic genetic code of the Kiwi boats. But, by rule, the teams went their separate ways in December 2012. The boat answering the guns in 2013 is an Italian reinvention.

Looking back on his decision to jump into the fray and recommit to the time, the management headaches and the extraordinary expenses, Bertelli recognized many motivations. Foremost, he said, "No Italian team was challenging. The Italian Challenger of Record had withdrawn its entry, and it was important

to bring Italian sailing back to the position it always enjoyed internationally, and in the America's Cup in particular. Also, there were great expectations in a comeback of Luna Rossa. Over the years our team has won the affection and support of a very wide audience, and it has become a kind of Italian national team. I was also driven by a concern that skipping one Cup would have meant accumulating a huge technical delay. It would have made it more difficult to challenge for the following Cup."

Luna Rossa skipper Massimiliano "Max" Sirena has "Cup fever" as surely as anyone, it seems. He recalled winning the Louis Vuitton Cup in 2000 as a highlight of his life, but even greater than that was 2010, when Sirena was share crew for ORACLE Racing's successful trimaran. "More than winning the race, on that day I drank champagne from the Cup. It's a feeling hard to describe. I was 'drugged' for a week."

Past Luna Rossa challenges carried the colors of yacht clubs from the central west coast and then the northern coast of Italy. This time out, Bertelli said, "After challenging with the Yacht Club Punta and the Yacht Club Italiano, we have decided to challenge with the Circolo della Vela Sicilia, one of the oldest and most representative yacht clubs of Italian sailing. With this choice we wanted to underline and stress how much the presence of seamanship and sailing traditions on our peninsula—from the Liguria to the Venezia Giulia regions—is widespread and diverse."

LEFT: Team Luna Rossa Challenge during the launch of their AC72. ABOVE: Luna Rossa in front of their fans in Venice, Italy.

the requirement to correct simultaneously for the distortion in a television lens—in a single zoom, it is possible to go from 10 percent pincushion distortion to 10 percent barrel distortion. Don't forget to add inertial sensors to correct for those college games, where the cameras are mounted on the stands, and when the kids get to rockin' and so do the stands.

But that is easy compared to taking the AC LiveLine bundle of technologies out of the relatively controlled, fixed world, moving it to the harsh environment of salt water, boats, and helicopters, and painting electronic lines on the water with a positioning tolerance of only 2 centimeters. Then consider the complexities of writing integrated code to correct simultaneously for the curvature of the Earth. No one expected immediate perfection, but early glitches and all, the system the sailors call "Stanware" clicked into place so quickly and with such precision that, suddenly, the Race Committee and the umpires wanted to use it too.

With its 2-centimeter tolerance, AC LiveLine can catch a boat that makes a premature start, and the Race Committee can penalize it with confidence. Even with the much slower boats of old, eyeballs could make mistakes. With AC72s moving at startling speeds, the eyeball would be too twentieth century.

Umpires, accustomed to chasing the racers in motorboats, eyeballing encounters, and signaling rules infractions by waving flags, now had tools that removed the judgment from their calls and eliminated guesswork that once seemed inevitable. For example, there is an imaginary circle around each turning mark, and that circle can be critical. The first boat to enter it gains the right-of-way for rounding and probably gains the lead on the next leg. But you won't be surprised to hear that, in the past, sailors and even umpires often disagreed as to the position of an imaginary circle on the water. The new electronics package removes the guesswork.

In 2013, the entire racecourse is dynamic, managed electronically, with Principal Race Officer John Craig adjusting the length of each race—longer or shorter—to suit an assigned schedule. Instead of buoys tethered to anchors, marks are boats with geopositioning capability that stay in one spot, or move, according to the master plan. Course boundaries and protest and penalty communications all are integrated into a package of software and hardware that at this point is too expensive and complex for ordinary sailing contests.

AC**L**iveLine

AC45 LiveLine System

OPPOSITE: Stan Honey hardwiring a prototype of the AC LiveLine system in his home workshop. • ABOVE: Principal Race Officer John Craig observing the AC LiveLine race data onboard a race committee boat during a match-race qualifier in San Francisco. To fit network television schedules, Craig often had to change the length of the course on the fly to ensure races would end reliably on time.

The America's Cup has a long tradition of technological trickle down, however. It will take a few years, but key elements of the package will eventually find their way to other high-end racecourses. What began as a determination to make sailing understandable on TV has gone beyond. But, returning to basics, the proof of concept is the human reaction to what Honey likes to call "augmented reality." There are cameras in the air and on the boats. The sailors are wired for sound, and for the first time they are forbidden to turn off their mics. Technology makes it crystal clear who is ahead and who is behind. It is now perfectly normal for people at the races to watch the race as the boats come near. And then, as the boats speed away, spray flying, the audience turns to study the race on TV or a tablet, where even an expert sailor can see and comprehend so much more.

Much was promised when the America's Cup came to San Francisco Bay. Given some of the most reliable winds in the world, it is reasonable to believe that this place can deliver the scheduling reliability that a television sport requires. With its open shorelines and surrounding hills, the bay fulfills the dream of "stadium sailing" for the largest live audience in the history of the sport. And given the bay's natural beauty, the cameras love it. So do visitors, including those who are drawn here because the Bay Area, from Silicon Valley to the Napa Valley, is a dynamo of innovation. What happens to all that AC LiveLine data? Why, it is streamed live, open source, to any geek who wants to play with it. That is the ethos of the 34th America's Cup.

ALPHABET SOUP: THE ACRM & ACEA

Two new organizations, the ACEA, America's Cup Event Authority, and the ACRM, America's Cup Race Management, developed out of months of meetings and late-night sessions. It was a time spent studying flip books and drawing boxes on whiteboards to illustrate areas of responsibility for the 34th America's Cup and, it was hoped, beyond.

The ACEA is responsible for running the America's Cup, and the ACRM is responsible for running the races for the America's Cup and the ACWS. In corporate terms, the ACEA is a profit and loss organization, managing the rights and seeking partnerships, sponsors, and revenue. The ACRM's job of running the racing program is purely sporting. It has no commercial role.

The fundamental premise of the ACRM is that it will stage its races and make its umpire calls on behalf of the event, independently, not as an interested agent of the defense. There has never been such a structure before. The ACRM's funding comes from the ACEA, as the only possible source, but how it manages the racing is its own business. The financing was structured so that the ACRM's chief executive officer, the multitalented Iain Murray, could be his own man, acting without fear of arbitrary reprisal. It's a far cry from the days when the yacht club that held the trophy would put its race committee on the water and run the races and name its own protest committee. The America's Cup long ago outgrew the capabilities of any yacht club for hands-on management.

Murray was a popular choice for the role. He emerged in the 1980s as a champion skiff racer and went on to design and sail the Australian Cup defender, *Kookaburra III*, that lost to Dennis Conner in 1987. By turns designer, boatbuilder, and waterfront developer, Murray brought with him a straight-shooting, no-nonsense reputation that perfectly fit his role at ACRM.

ABOVE: Ian Murray, the ACRM's chief executive officer, brought with him a wealth of America's Cup experience as well as a no-nonsense attitude that helped establish a clear separation between America's Cup Race Management and the defending syndicate, a separation absent from past America's Cups.

The America's Cup long ago outgrew the capabilities of any yacht club for hands-on management.

The race management system was fine-tuned as the America's Cup World Series tours passed through the UK, Portugal, Italy, and the United States. The immediate success of the AC45s, with their speed and visual thrills, set new standards for what Coutts began to call "stadium racing" for a live audience. Principal Race Officer John Craig, a onetime Olympic coach who had spent eleven years managing races on San Francisco Bay for the St. Francis Yacht Club, experimented with short races (then, even shorter races) and novel configurations.

RED BULL YOUTH AMERICA'S CUP

The Red Bull Youth America's Cup, a worthy new initiative of the 34th America's Cup, gives talented young sailors from around the world the opportunity to try their hand at America's Cup–style sailing—something Cup sailors of previous generations could generally not experience until much later in their careers. In the past, an Olympic medal was typically the passport for sailors wishing to graduate into the America's Cup. The new initiative, backed by the well-known Austrian energy drink manufacturer, aims to provide an alternative and more direct pathway into sailing's ultimate event.

The initiative is close to the heart of Jimmy Spithill, ORACLE TEAM USA skipper, who, uniquely, was given his break as an America's Cup skipper at age nineteen, when Australian Syd Fischer put him on the wheel of *Young Australia*, which went on to compete in the 30th America's Cup, in 2000, in New Zealand. At thirty, Spithill became the youngest skipper to win the America's Cup with BMW ORACLE Racing's victory over *Alinghi 5* in the 33rd America's Cup.

"I think this is one of the most exciting developments in the America's Cup in a very long time," said Spithill. "Breaking into the America's Cup is hard. I was very fortunate to get a break with the *Young Australia* team, which allowed me to get into the game and get noticed. But this is going to give many more young sailors the same type of opportunity."

Traditionally, the America's Cup is where racing sailors get to compete at the pinnacle of their careers, but the more demanding physical nature of the 34th America's Cup catamarans means that in years to come the average age of crews may be lower—especially so if a pool of eager new talent is waiting in the wings.

BELOW: Red Bull Youth America's Cup selection series, February 2013.

ABOVE: Practicing alongside Luna Rossa Challenge proved essential to getting to grips with the learning curve. As Dean Barker of Emirates Team New Zealand explained, "Until you are forced into a race environment you just do not realize how hard these boats are to manage."

THE RIGHT CATS FOR THE MATCH

The story of the San Francisco America's Cup is a story of bold decisions. Multihulls historically have been regarded as too slow through maneuvers for the elegant sparring of a proper match race. Ample tests were conducted before the decision was made to contest the Cup in catamarans. The decision was controversial, and yes, something of the old game has been left behind, but much more has been brought forward. The 34th America's Cup will provide the ultimate test. To the objection that catamarans maneuver too slowly for match racing, Coutts replied, "That's because the right catamarans for match racing haven't been designed yet." As soon as the new breed of cats hit the water, it was clear that their time through maneuvers, from full speed to a return to full speed, was almost identical to the maneuvering times for the monohull IACC boats last raced in Valencia in 2007. The difference—the premium now on minimizing maneuvers—comes about because the other guy is going so fast while you're turning that you just can't give him any gimmes.

At the same time that catamarans were being trialed for match racing, the courses were shortened and constrained and moved closer and closer to shore, closer and closer to a potential audience, closer and closer to that day in 2012 when San Francisco's first America's Cup World Series wrapped up in the waters of the 2013 America's Cup match. Coutts, the cheers of the crowd still ringing in his ears, proclaimed yet another step complete, using words you've heard before, "Proof of concept!" The man who has won more America's Cup races than anyone else was pumped. The opening act of the 34th America's Cup was getting rave reviews. Coutts had struggled through negativity, negativity, negativity, and now it was all fireworks. Curmudgeon-veterans of "the real America's Cup" were, even at that moment, adjusting their opinions in his favor.

Now it all comes together, complete with surprises. When the AC72 rule was devised, it didn't seem that the boats produced by the formulas would be true foilers—their hulls lifting clear of the water to minimize resistance—but, in 2013, hydrofoils are as key to cutting-edge development as wings. AC72s in 2013 are foiling, or "flying," and gaining enough extra speed to force Principal Race Officer John Craig to adjust his racecourse.

"Sorry, John" is how that goes. Apparently, when you set out to change everything, everything changes. At the 34th America's Cup, sailing stakes its claim on the twenty-first century. ◄

OPPOSITE: Emirates Team New Zealand's second AC72 hit the water months before ORACLE TEAM USA's or Artemis Racing's. • TOP: After many delays, Artemis Racing launched their big cat in early November 2012. • ABOVE: For those who argued that multihulls couldn't possibly have the presence and majesty of monohulls, the launch of Luna Rossa's AC72 was an eye-opener.

PAGES 216–217: ORACLE TEAM USA exhibiting the essence of the America's Cup: speed.

MYSTIC SEAPORT

THE MUSEUM OF AMERICA AND THE SEA

THROUGH IMAGES OF EVERY AMERICA'S CUP from 1885 to 1992, the Rosenfeld Collection celebrates the legacy of sailing's ultimate race. Nowhere else is the drama of the Cup captured so brilliantly, or the power and beauty of wind, sail, and sea so artfully documented.

With nearly one million photographs taken over two generations, the Rosenfeld Collection at Mystic Seaport is the largest single collection of maritime photography in the world—a true showcase of the art of the boat, and a testament to the allure of the America's Cup.

INSIGHT
EDITIONS

PO Box 3088
San Rafael, CA 94912
www.insighteditions.com

Find us on Facebook: www.facebook.com/InsightEditions
Follow us on Twitter: @insighteditions

Library of Congress Cataloging-in-Publication Data available.

ISBN: 978-1-60887-206-0

COLOPHON
PUBLISHER: Raoul Goff
CO-PUBLISHERS: John Owen & Michael Madden
ART DIRECTOR: Chrissy Kwasnik
PRODUCTION MANAGER: Anna Wan
ASSOCIATE EDITOR: Dustin Jones

INSIGHT EDITIONS would like to thank Louisa Watrous, Judith Dunham,
Peter Rusch, Sean McNeill, Tim Jeffery, Petra Carran, Francesco Longanesi Cattani,
Warren Douglas, Laurent du Roure, Alexandra Peyron, Bruno Troublé, and Larry Keating.

 and all other related indicia are the intellectual property of the America's Cup
Event Authority. © 2013 America's Cup Event Authority.

 REPLANTED PAPER
Insight Editions, in association with Roots of Peace, will plant two trees for each tree
used in the manufacturing of this book. Roots of Peace is an internationally renowned
humanitarian organization dedicated to eradicating land mines worldwide and
converting war-torn lands into productive farms and wildlife habitats. Roots of Peace
will plant two million fruit and nut trees in Afghanistan and provide farmers there
with the skills and support necessary for sustainable land use.

Manufactured in Hong Kong by Insight Editions

10 9 8 7 6 5 4 3 2 1

PHOTOGRAPHER BIOS

CARLO BORLENGHI is the team photographer for Luna Rossa
Challenge and winner of numerous awards, including the Marin
Skubin prize, the Marina Di Pescara Award, and the Omega
prize. He lives in Milan, Italy.

CHRIS CAMERON is the official photographer for Emirates
Team New Zealand, and his work can be found in specialist
sailing magazines worldwide. He lives in Auckland, New
Zealand.

DANIEL FORSTER has been covering the America's Cup since
1977. His work has been published in every major nautical
magazine in Europe, New Zealand, Australia, and the United
States, as well as in general interest magazines, including *TIME*.
He lives in Newport, Rhode Island.

GUILAIN GRENIER is team photographer for ORACLE TEAM
USA. Grenier is published in nautical magazines around the
world, including *Yachting World* and *Seahorse*. He currently
lives in Marseille, France.

SHARON GREEN is known for her spectacular *Ultimate Sailing*
calendars, and is currently working on a highly anticipated
collection of her finest yacht racing photographs. She lives in
Santa Barbara, California.

Former staff photographer at the *Washington Star* and the
Los Angeles Times, **BOB GRIESER** is a longtime contributor to
Sailing Magazine, and currently shoots for Louis Vuitton. He
lives in San Diego, California.

GILLES MARTIN-RAGET is the official photographer for the
34th America's Cup, and is frequently published in many
prominent sailing magazines, including *Yachting World* and
Nautique. He lives in Marseille, France.

DAN NERENY'S marine photography has graced yachting
publications worldwide. He has covered twelve America's Cups
and is the official photographer of the New York Yacht Club.

SANDER VAN DER BORCH is team photographer for Artemis
Racing. With an extensive background in regatta sailing, Sander
is known for capturing interesting angles and intense situations
on the racecourse. He currently lives in the Hague.